The Word
in Action

ROSS MACKENZIE

The Word
in Action

The Acts of the Apostles for Our Time

JOHN KNOX PRESS / Atlanta, Georgia

Library of Congress Cataloging in Publication Data

Mackenzie, Ross, 1927-
   The word in action.
   Includes bibliographical references.
   1. Bible. N. T. Acts—Criticism, interpretation, etc. I. Title.
BS2625.2.M33   226'.6'07   72-6968
ISBN 0-8042-9088-1

© John Knox Press 1973
PRINTED IN THE UNITED STATES OF AMERICA
51-8088 Second Printing 1974

The Covenant Life Curriculum suggests that there are at least three different avenues by which to enter into a study of the Christian faith. You can start with the Bible and see what it says and where it leads you. You can start with the church, God's people, to learn what God has led and is leading them to be and say and do. Or you can start with the daily concerns of life, to see what the Christian faith can tell you about faithful living in the twentieth century. In each case the Bible is basic, the church is involved, and the truth must relate to daily life.

This study is one of three "Bible Studies for Modern Man" for use in 1973 and beyond. Together they offer study materials for an entire year or more, though each can be studied alone. This text, *The Word in Action*, is a study of the Book of Acts that relates the problems of the early church and the solutions it found to them to the life of our churches today. *Exercises in Interpreting Scripture*, by John Frederick Jansen, provides adults and youth with basic principles of Biblical interpretation and with experience in applying these to four key Biblical passages. *The Covenants in Faith and History*, by Stephen Szikszai, is an overview of the entire Bible through a survey of God's covenants with his people in the Old and New Testaments.

The teacher's book, *Leader's Guide to Bible Studies for Modern Man*, gives session-by-session help on leading adults and youth in the study of all three texts.

The denominations that publish these books have produced three other year-long Bible courses for adult-youth study. *The Mighty Acts of God* surveys the entire Bible from Genesis to Revelation in considerable detail (448 pages). *From Bondage to Freedom*, by four different authors, combines in one volume studies of Exodus, Isaiah 40–66, John, and Galatians. The 1970 Bible study resources appeared in three separate and smaller volumes: *Common Sense and the Gospel* (a study of Wisdom literature: Job, Proverbs, etc.); *The Gospel for God's People* (Matthew); and *Living the Gospel* (First Peter). For all of these, detailed teacher's guides are available.

Also part of the Covenant Life Curriculum are three series of studies on the history, doctrine, and life of the church, and three studies on Christian ethics. For further details on any of these, contact any sponsoring denomination: Associate Reformed Presbyterian Church, Cumberland Presbyterian Church, Moravian Church in America, Presbyterian Church in the United States, Reformed Church in America, and (affiliate) The Evangelical Covenant Church of America; or Curriculum Promotion, Box 1176, Richmond, Virginia 23209.

Contents

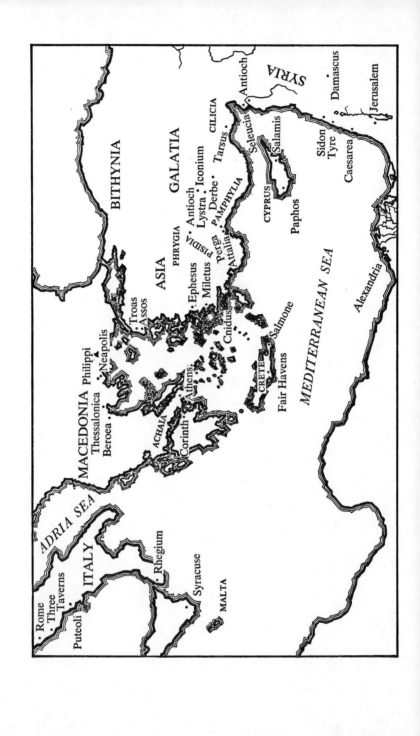

Luke — writer of Acts

1 gentile convert

1

The Spirit Fills the World
Acts 1—2

THE BOOK OF ACTS has a single emphasis: *proclaiming the gospel of the risen Christ through the power of the Spirit*. We could speak of Acts as "the history of the Holy Spirit in the early church." A modern writer commenting on the book describes thus the relation between the Gospels and Acts: "The gospel tells how God 'visited and redeemed his people' by sending his Son, Jesus Christ. The Acts tells how this event became 'a light to lighten the Gentiles' through the witness of the Spirit-filled church." [1]

The abrupt ending of the last chapter suggests that the climax of Acts is to be found *outside* the book, in the continuing activity of the Spirit in the world. This helps to explain the direction followed in our present study. We shall try to find the meaning of the Acts of the Apostles for our time. Of course, we shall "play fair" with Acts and honestly try to see what it says. But we shall always do so mindful of our own world, a world in which some find happiness but which often confronts us with revolution, violence, and tragic dilemmas.

What follows, then, is basically a setting out of what *once* took place, and an attempt to find out what that can mean for those who belong to "the way of Christ" in our day. Thus each chapter begins by examining a section in Acts. Constantly we shall ask: What was the secret of their lively, infectious enthusiasm? How did that new community grow?

At the end of each chapter questions will be raised for thought and discussion. Naturally these will not deal with every possible issue related to the passage. Your own creative study of Acts may well push you beyond the questions to problems and concerns that affect you at the moment of study.

Clearly, then, this is not a commentary on the text of Acts. It is a running attempt to bring out of an ancient book insights which may guide us today as people of God. And though at times the questions raised may be hard ones for many of us to deal with (because they compel us to ask how we understand the gospel in our turbulent world), we shall never understand the truth that is Christ until we face the issues of *our* world in the grace of Christ and the power of the Spirit.

THE CHIEF THEMES OF THE BOOK, 1:1-4

In the first few verses of Acts the chief themes of the book are set out.

1) *Continuity.* In his first book (the Gospel of Luke) the author tells us what Jesus *began* to do. The second book (Acts) tells us what Jesus *continued* to do in the midst of his apostles through the Spirit. The life of the apostolic church continued what was started by Jesus.

The framers of the Scots Confession (1560) used a strange phrase when they said that there has been a "Kirk in all ages since Adam." They meant there has never been a time when God was not calling a people to himself. In a real sense the church of Acts is in continuity with the people of God from the beginning. Thus the first Christians thought that they were one with the covenant people of old, Israel, and in their journeys the earliest missionaries gravitated toward the synagogues of the Jews. Usually they were warmly welcomed; only at a later date did bitter divisions separate them.

To belong to the church is thus to belong to a *catholic* community (the Greek *katholikos* means "throughout the whole world"). The church is one and the same and continuous in every age.

Acts tells us of the early life of the people of the new covenant. Small in number at first (120 in all—see 1:15; where no book is named in Biblical citations, Acts is to be understood), by the end

TIME CHART

A time chart may help us to keep our bearings in the study of Acts. The dates are approximate.

	A.D.		ACTS
30	30	The resurrection and ascension of Jesus	1:6–11
		Appointment of the Seven	6:1–7
		Death of Stephen	7:54—8:1
	34–36	Conversion of Paul	9:1–22
40	37–39	Paul's first visit to Jerusalem	9:26–30
	43–44	In Antioch	11:19–26
	45–49	Paul's first journey	13:1—14:28
	49	Council at Jerusalem	15:1–35
50	49–52	Paul's second journey 1 and 2 Thessalonians	15:36—18:22
	53–58	Paul's third journey Galatians, 1 Corinthians 2 Corinthians, Romans	18:23—21:17
	58	Paul's arrest in Jerusalem	21:27–36
60	58–60	Caesarea	23:23—26:32
	60–61	Appointment of Festus	24:27
	60–61	Paul's journey to Rome	27:1—28:16
	61–63	Imprisonment in Rome Colossians, Philippians Ephesians, Philemon	28:30–31

of the account they had become a numberless fellowship. The "catholic church" in this sense is simply humanity in all its diversity beginning to be restored to unity in Jesus Christ.

So the line stretches out from the beginning. In Paul chanting in jail, Perpetua and Felicity dying in the arena at Carthage, Augustine teaching in northern Africa, Columba celebrating the liturgy on the island of Iona, Luther standing firm at Worms, Theresa blending mysticism and common sense at Avila, Zinzendorf preaching his "religion of the heart" in Herrnhut, and Niemöller witnessing to Christ in a concentration camp—in these and their kin the acts of apostolic men and women continued and still continue to be seen.

2) *The preaching of salvation.* To belong to the church is also to belong to an *evangelical* community (the Greek *euangelion* means "good news" or "gospel"). A second theme of the book is the preaching of salvation by the apostles. The early church existed to witness to what God had done in Jesus Christ.

With the ascension of Christ, of which we shall shortly read, Jesus was no longer present as he had been before. He was now *exalted* Lord. But who was this Lord who was exalted? He was the same as before, still deeply involved in human pain and need. This same caring Lord was yet present through the words of those who proclaimed his gospel and (as we shall see) in the life and worship of the new community. To speak of the church as the "body" of Christ simply means that through the community of his people in the world this true "man for others," Jesus Christ, becomes accessible to our need and available for our healing. In the words of Erasmus, a sixteenth-century writer: "By a Carpenter mankind was created and made, and by a Carpenter meet it was that man should be repaired."

Preaching was thus the witness of the early church to the living and creating Christ. He stood, they thought, behind every word the apostles proclaimed. Paul expressed this idea in his Letter to Timothy when he said: "the Lord stood by me and gave me strength to proclaim his word fully." (2 Tim. 4:17)

The theme of apostolic preaching varied, but its heart and soul was Christ (8:5), the kingdom of God (28:31), the message of salvation (13:26), and the word of grace (14:3). The gospel was the announcement that Christ had come into history to stop the processes by which human life is ruined. It was a revolutionary gospel because it involved the conversion of the mind and outlook of the individual. It penetrated not only to the inmost parts of man but also to the inmost parts of society, and it fashioned man and society to the true beauty of the new creation in Christ. This is still the gospel for us!

3) *The spontaneous activity of the Holy Spirit.* A third theme to be found in Actss is the gift and activity of the Spirit. The first Christians thought of themselves as the fellowship of the Spirit because he made the apostolic church the infectiously exciting reality it was. The early church was not an institution produced by human ingenuity. It was a "happening," an event brought about through the power of the Spirit.

When we lose the idea of spontaneity and freedom, we have lost touch with the real meaning of the church. The lively Christian is aware that life is a matter of being constantly sensitive and responsive to the Spirit. The church as the fellowship of the Spirit always must be looking for fresh ways to show how God is at work in disclosing new truth about himself or deepening love in all human relationships. We can recognize these early Christians as kin to us only if we come to share in their freedom to be creative and imaginative in obeying the voice of the Spirit.

At Pentecost Christ bestowed the Spirit on the apostles, as he had promised. By this gift they were equipped for preaching and for building up the church in the face of attack (see 4:31; 9:31). Acts has many more passages referring to the Spirit than any other book of the New Testament. As was suggested earlier, some for this reason even call it "The Acts of the Spirit."

The Preparation of the Apostles, 1:1–5

The prologue of the Acts speaks also about the preparation of the apostles for what was to come. They needed first *the assurance of the presence of Christ* (1:3). Such a task as Luke describes, that of bringing the gospel from Jerusalem "to the end of the earth," could be undertaken only in the confidence that Jesus Christ was with them.

Many people today, if asked about the meaning of Jesus, would think of the past—of his teachings and example above all. But the first Christians began with his presence, not his past. Faith meant a personal relation of a man or a woman to God, of person to Person. It was a personal communing with God.

Second, the apostles *had to learn more about the kingdom of God*. It is one thing to say or believe that Jesus is Lord. It is another thing to show in our lives that where God rules over the human heart, there the kingdom of love is established.

Third, the apostles needed *a power or energy that was greater than their own*. The prologue ends, therefore, with the promise that the Spirit will come to them. Two words are characteristically used about the Spirit in the New Testament. One is "wind." Samuel Rutherford once said: "Seamen cannot create the wind, but they can hoist their sails to welcome it." The earliest church was "on the move" because it was impelled by the Spirit to go where it would never have dared go on its own.

The other word is "power." The Spirit is the spirit of energy. And from the beginning the Spirit has given power to people— power to respond to the love of God in Christ, power to grow to our full stature as human beings, power to serve Christ with a warm new charity in factories, senate houses, schools, and homes. Do we stop here? The Spirit has still greater power, if only we are ready to welcome it; power to overcome all the sinful forces that alienate men and women from each other in family, society, or world—injustice, poverty, and hatred.

THE ASCENSION, 1:6–11

Since Luke twice describes the ascension (Luke 24:50–53; Acts 1:9) and refers to it many other times (as in Acts 2:33–35, 3:21, etc.), what it meant was obviously very important to him.

God and his power are real. This is the meaning of the resurrection. When the apostles first preached "Jesus and the resurrection" (Acts 17:18), they were saying that all that Jesus ever was and all the life and love they had ever known in him wasn't dead and buried. He was still with them, the living, loving, present Lord. He was all that he ever had been, but more, because death could never sever the bond between him and his people. This is what they proclaimed all the time. The resurrection meant that Christ was present with his followers, though in a new way.

The ascension is Luke's way of saying in pictorial language that the resurrection appearances of Jesus were now ended. To say that Christ has ascended is also to say that he is the universal Lord, dwelling at the very center of reality, reigning in such a way that by his Spirit he empowers us to live as true human beings.

At the heart of the passage is the command of Jesus to the apostles to bear witness to him throughout the world. (Compare 1:22; 2:32; 3:15, etc.) The circle was to be opened out so widely that the preaching that began in the narrow confines of Jerusalem would end in the capital of the empire. And from Rome roads led out to all the world.

The Waiting Period, 1:12–14

Nostalgia means homesickness, a longing to go back to one's roots; it means a love for a place where a commitment was once made, a difficult decision faced, or a deep affection expressed. For the apostles there was something of this nostalgia after the sudden, sharp changes of Easter and its aftermath were over. Perhaps they felt deserted. So they went back from the mount called Olivet to Jerusalem. There Jesus had undergone his agony of commitment and of decision, of facing the full meaning of what it is to love the world.

They came to an upper room, presumably the same room where Jesus had eaten supper with them before his death. They were eleven in number, the ones whom Jesus had chosen from a much larger number to be with him and to preach. To them Jesus had disclosed the secrets of his kingdom. There in the room they joined in continuous prayer.

Waiting is not always a bad thing. At times in the life of the church the best thing to do is to sit still and plot the future. For the apostles no clear line of action was open at that moment. So they simply waited.

THE NUMBER OF THE TWELVE COMPLETED, 1:15–26

Jesus had commissioned the Twelve to be his companions and the bearers of his message. The death of Judas (here described) had reduced the number by one, so at Peter's prompting the number was brought up to twelve again. The number itself may have been intended to suggest Israel (which according to tradition had twelve tribes). The emphasis on the number implied that a renewal was taking place among the people of God, and that the first apostles had a crucial part to play in opening the door of a new age.

The apostle had one supreme qualification, and from this we can learn something about our own discipleship. He was a witness to Christ's resurrection. It was on this witness that the community of faith was (and still is) built. Yet it is not the Twelve alone who are witnesses. So we conclude:

The starting point of the Christian movement is the encounter in which men and women truly meet the risen Christ.

With this encounter the gathering and renewal of the people of God begin.

The Christian community does not exist for itself but must turn to the world as the sphere in which the new life in Christ comes to expression.

PENTECOST, 2:1–13

With Pentecost we come to the next step in what is really the preparation for the acts of the apostles.

It seemed to these first Christians that they were living on the lip of a new era. All that had been dimly glimpsed in bygone ages about the purposes of God was becoming brilliantly clear in the light of a new dawn. Long, long before, a process had begun which would finally usher in the rule of God over the hearts of all people. The process had begun at the very beginning of things. It was discerned in the calling of Abraham, in the joyful and tragic experiences of the exodus, and in the exile of Israel in Babylon. It came to supreme expression in the birth, life, death, and resurrection of Jesus Christ.

In a way Pentecost was the climax of this process. Let us try to see what it meant and what it means. The Pentecost experience tells us, first, that *a new age has come*. In the past history of God's people, the hope had often been expressed that a new day would come when, as Isaiah put it, the glory of the Lord would be revealed (Isa. 40:5), or, as Joel said, God would pour out his Spirit in abundance (Joel 2:28—29). Pentecost means "this is the day!"

Perhaps more of us have had this kind of experience than we realize, but we have misunderstood it because we have thought of it in too "religious" a way. We may have had an insight in which our whole being was lifted to a new level of reality. Or we may have found an unfamiliar beauty. Or we may have come to understand a mysterious truth or come to know the love that underlies the sum of things—the love that moves the sun and also the hearts of even the simplest human beings. On these occasions it dawns on us that something new is happening in our lives. Pentecost was profoundly like that, but the same Spirit is still at work, conforming us to Christ, bringing out the best within us. The Spirit is still (in the wrds of the Nicene Creed) the "Giver of Life."

Pentecost also means that *the separation dividing people from one another can be taken away*. The Babel story (Gen. 11:1–10) explained a complex problem in the family of man—estrangement and division. The "confusion of tongues" was thought to be a divine judgment. Pentecost means that human history has decisively moved to a different stage. The gulfs dividing people from one another can in principle be bridged.

The Galileans (2:7), i.e., the followers of Jesus, have a word that makes sense in every language. Isaiah had written that God would one day speak to his people "by men of strange lips and with an alien tongue." (Isa. 28:11) Pentecost means "This is the day!"

Something else of interest strikes us about the events of Pente-cost: *the conduct of those who are filled by the Spirit is often mistaken for madness.* The disciples on the day of Pentecost were accused of being crazy with drink. They talked a lot. They did things they would not have done normally. They laughed. They were excited. They felt a glow inside them. But the joy with which they were filled was no pumped-up enthusiasm. It flowed from the Spirit and gave them a verve that could not be tempered.

An observer of the early church said in criticism that Christians were "illiterate yokels" who "let out some astounding statements." But this ecstatic joy is one of the fruits of the Spirit (Gal. 5:22—23). It is one of the ultimate distinctions between a Christian and a non-Christian. The writer of Hebrews speaks of Jesus as the one "who for the joy that was set before him endured the cross, de-spising the shame." (Heb. 12:2) A cross or a pain or a burden can be endured with a cold bravery, or it can be accepted with joy. The apostles knew that if the new age was at hand it would demand sacrifice and constancy in sacrifice. Without the Spirit they might have faced it with fear or nervousness; but with the Spirit they had the joy of God himself. There is a French play in which the following dialogue occurs:

> *Brother Trophimus.* Inertia is the only vice, Master Erasmus;
> and the only virtue is . . .
> *Erasmus.* What?
> *Brother Trophimus.* Enthusiasm![2]

The apostles would likely have understood.

The Results of Apostolic Preaching, 2:37–47

The account of the Spirit in the earlier passage is followed immediately by the first sermon recorded in Acts (2:14–36). Read it over and outline it for yourself. The sermon shows us what was central to apostolic preaching: Christ, and more particularly the cross (2:23) and the resurrection (2:24).

The cross reveals the limit to which the Servant who is also Redeemer has gone in his total self-emptying. The cross means that Jesus has come into the disorder of human life to be not only "the man for others" but also *God for man,* meeting sin, accepting all it entails, and breaking its power. The cross is therefore the means of access to real life. But the work of salvation does not end with the cross. It is brought to fulfillment in the resurrection. In a way that defies description Jesus becomes present to faith as "risen." Two results of Peter's preaching are described.

1) *Repentance is the first* (2:37). True proclamation of the gospel calls for a personal response like this. Repentance does not mean futilely beating our heads with our hands in guilt and remorse. It means rather a turning of our whole selves to the source of our new life in God.

Repentance is a serious thing; it need not be a solemn thing. It does not mean strangling our humor but reaching out to people with our joy. It does not mean becoming somber; it means discovering the tenderness and closeness and pleasure and love and depth and freedom of the life which we find in Christ.

2) *Baptism, the gift of the Spirit, and the fellowship of the Spirit.* The verses which conclude the chapter (2:41–47) describe the irreducible minimum of what makes the church. It is the people of God called into being by the Spirit; a society of those who recieve and believe the word of the apostles; the place of the sacraments; and a community of men and women who have been so overwhelmingly changed by Christ that they seek to express their new life in ways which show how deeply they feel they belong to one another (see especially 2:45). Even outsiders were impressed by the charm of their life together.

A key to the life of the new community was "the breaking of bread," or Eucharist. (This is a technical term. It simply means "thanksgiving.") The risen Christ was known (as he was to the Emmaus travelers—Luke 24—and as he is known still today) in the breaking of bread. In the simple act of eating and drinking at his supper, a bond of affection bound and binds one to one another, and a life is experienced unlike any other kind of living in the world.

FOR THOUGHT AND DISCUSSION

There follow two passages from modern writers. Think about what they mean to you and be prepared to discuss them in light of the insights you have gained from the study of Acts so far.

> For the disciples during those first shattering hours, Jesus had become a memory. He was someone they had known and loved and lost.
>
> They had shared with him a depth of living they had not guessed before. All their hopes for a better way of life were centered in him, and lost with him—buried and sealed in the tomb.
>
> It was all over. They had been quickened by a vision of what life could be, but now they must face life as it was. Back to reality!
>
> And then IT happened. It came to them—rather, as they could only describe it, HE came to them.
>
> *The life they had known and shared was not buried with him but alive in them.* Jesus was not a dead memory but a living presence.
>
> John A. T. Robinson, *But That I Can't Believe!* [3]

Put in your own words what the writer means by saying that the risen Christ whom the disciples had known was "alive in them." Do you agree with him? Do members of your congregation (or study group) know Jesus more as a dead memory than as a living presence? In what ways do we experience the risen Christ in our midst? What is the relation between your church and the risen Jesus Christ?

> The church is made up of ordinary men and women, yet is, by God's action, his Son's body on earth, living his life, doing his will, knowing his glory. And, as his body, it is here in the world to be the instrument of God's purpose for the world.

Buildings, clergy, seminaries, and social responsibility with, as the other side of the coin, social respectability—are all things that we take for granted for the church. We cannot conceive of the church existing without them. If we did not have to raise money to build new buildings and to maintain old ones, if we did not have to train and maintain the clergy and undertake social service in our own country and elsewhere, what would members of the church do? What did the early church do when it did not have to trouble about these things? It converted the Roman Empire.

Of course, we need these things in some form. An organization cannot exist without some kind of structure. The church, no less than the family, needs some kind of institution. But it can be of the flimsiest. The church—and the family—can do without a building. The church—and the family—can live in tents, can be on the move. The church—and the family—can exist without its official leaders. A family still exists when the parents are dead. The church—and the family—can be outcast and outlawed. The only thing without which the church—and the family—cannot survive is a way of life, a bond of affection, expressed in custom, tradition, and ceremony, which for the church comes from the life that Jesus lived with men. But, though it needs some structure, the church, like the family, is not primarily an institution. It is essentially people living a life together: the people of God living the life of Christ.

Mark Gibbs and T. Ralph Morton, *God's Frozen People*[4]

What do you think the writers are saying is the only thing without which the church cannot survive? Do you think they have exaggerated? How do you think the average congregation would react to such a challenge? How should it? What help do the authors give you in understanding what Acts says about the earliest community of believers?

Begin .

The Boldness of the New Community

Acts 3:1—5:11

R EFERRING TO the great age of English writing, John Keats
spoke in one of his letters about "the indescribable gusto of
the Elizabethan voice." But for sheer zest nothing can match the
Galilean voice, the voice of those who belonged to the first apostolic
community. Luke speaks in his narrative of their "boldness" (4:13).
The word suggests a refusal to be beaten down, a vivacious living
out of the new life. Paul himself gives us a quickly sketched but
graphic pen-picture of the young church in action:

> We are in difficulties on all sides, but never cornered; we see
> no answer to our problems, but never despair; we have been
> persecuted, but never deserted; knocked down, but never killed;
> always, wherever we may be, we carry with us in our body the
> death of Jesus, so that the life of Jesus, too, may always be
> seen in our body. (2 Cor. 4:8–10, *The Jerusalem Bible*) [1]

Conventional Christianity has often been a matter of living
tame lives and holding safe opinions. The earliest disciples knew
that if Jesus was Lord of the universe they would have to turn the
world the right way around.

THE POWER OF THE WORD, 3:1—4:37

No one had a stronger conviction of the power of God's word
than Martin Luther. In his *Table Talk* he once wrote with typical
bluntness: "God, with one sole word, moulded the whole world."

This was the conviction also of the apostles, and they held it even more strongly. The word which they preached as God's word in their day also is in our day capable of making the old new and the broken whole. It can mold communities of faith, hope, and love out of the raw materials of the lesser communities of ordinary daily life.

In Acts 3:1–4:37, there are three important and closely connected elements, each having to do in some way with the power of God's word expressed in the voice and life of the apostolic community. One is the sign or miracle of the healing of the lame man (3:1–10), the second in Peter's sermon (3:11–26) and the third, following the arrest of Peter and John, is the pattern of life of the new community (4:23–35). We can think of the relation between these ideas as a triangle with "word," "sign," and "community" as the three points.

1) One of the points of the triangle is *the preaching of the apostolic gospel*. The early church was quite convinced that when the gospel is proclaimed, God himself speaks. His Word is a powerful word. It gives life, it saves, and it heals. It teaches and illuminates.

2) The second point of the triangle is *the sign confirming the Word*. We find the same idea at the end of Mark's Gospel: "They went forth and preached everywhere, while the Lord worked with them and confirmed the message by the signs that attended it." (Mark 16:20) The miraculous healing of the lame man is to be understood as a sign confirming the truth and power of the apostolic gospel. To ask whether the miracle happened as described is really not the question for us. The story is told to show that the early church experienced in its own life signs that God was in control, the Lord of all life. To what extent do we share that experience?

3) The third point of the triangle is *the life of the community itself*. When the Word of God is preached, it arouses in many who hear it a response—faith. We come to faith through hearing. And we come to the new life in Christ through faith. The church is

thus a community of faith, the unique community in which the new life is even now beginning to be lived.

The three points of the triangle give us *insight into the meaning and life of the church today.*

The *preaching of the gospel* is still of dominant importance. It may be proclaimed or heard or understood in many ways: in worship, teaching, private conversation, or public discussion. We need the word which speaks to us about the kingdom of God. To quote Luther again (who saw all this so clearly): "one thing alone is essential, namely, the word of God by which we live." The word of the gospel tells us who we are. It shows us the goal to which God calls us. It links the community together.

To hear the word of God, to be a Christian, is above all things to belong to a people. To be "in the church" means to belong to a special kind of *community.* It is the company of those who, like the son in the parable, have come back to the waiting Father from the places where they were lost or afraid or lacking. Within this company we discover our real selves for the first time, and, even more important, we discover others in ourselves and ourselves in others. We discover how inextricably we are tied up in the bundle of life with all other human beings.

Within this community there are still clear *signs* that God is at work making the old new and the broken whole. The Eucharist is such a sign. The common loaf and the common cup are signs of a unity that is becoming realized among us. An ancient prayer (referring to grain growing on the hills) expresses the unity this way: "As this broken bread was scattered upon the hills, and was gathered together and made one, so let thy church be gathered together into thy kingdom from the ends of the earth." [2]

THE COMMUNITY CALLED INTO BEING THROUGH THE WORD, 4:23–31

Three events are reported prior to the account of the Christian community given in these verses. The first is the healing of the lame man (3:1–10).

This is followed by Peter's sermon (3:12–26). Read through the sermon and identify the names or activities which are attributed to Jesus in verses 13, 14, 15, 16, and 18. From these designations we learn something of the view which the first Christians held of Jesus. As servant, he imparts the grace of God to the nations, opening the eyes of the blind, liberating prisoners, and bringing *shalom* or that peace of God which is rooted in our innermost being. The consequence of this service for Jesus was to be debased, humbled, punished, and put to death. Jesus is this servant, this kind of Christ.

The third event described in these chapters is the arrest of Peter and John (4:1–4), and Peter's courageous and brilliant speech before the supreme council (4:5–22). Due to the Sanhedrin's fear of a popular rebellion, the two were released. With their return to their friends we see in greater detail the remarkable life of the earliest community of believers (4:23–37). Four characteristics of the community stand out.

1) *A community of prayer.* It is typical of Luke that he stresses the prayer that was so habitual a part of the life of the first Christians. The attitudes which they brought to their praying are informative.

First, they called on God as "Sovereign Lord" and "Maker of heaven and earth." The powerful council had threatened them, but there was a power greater than that of all who might gather against them (4:24).

Second, they knew that God had a purpose (4:25).

Third, they were confident that the word they proclaimed would be accompanied by deeds demonstrating God's power (4:30).

2) *A community of love.* A second characteristic of this young community was their oneness of heart and soul. An intimate friend of St. Bernard described the community founded at Clairvaux in the twelfth century as "a school of love, where the study of love is pursued, love's disputations held, love's questions answered." We must be on guard against romanticizing the early church, but for all its weaknesses it was a remarkable school of love, a community of oneness in Jesus Christ. All were one in the Lord, a community

of concord (which means literally "of one heart"—see 4:32).

3) *A community of economic sharing.* The emphasis on the sharing of possessions in 4:32–35 is impressive. "Every man for himself, and devil take the hindmost"—could a Christian ever say this? The young church tried an amazing experiment when they brought together their economic life and their life of prayer. They had everything in common, yet they respected the right to private property. They remembered Jesus' warnings about the dangers of wealth. The true riches of the disciples were the new life in the Spirit.

Jesus often warned his followers that the way in which money is used is a barometer of a man's real nature. Someone once said: "The sin of the world begins over this business of bread-getting." Who ought to have more insight than the Christian community into the getting and sharing of bread? At the center of its worship it breaks bread in remembering Christ, and it shares bread. There is a deep meaning here. Those who break bread together *sacramentally* must learn how to share *economically* with one another.

What would it mean for Christ's followers today to take this seriously? At the very least it might mean seeking the mind of Christ not only in drawing up confessions of faith but also in matters of work and wages.

4) *A community of grace.* The earliest church was also a community of grace (see 4:33). Its members had been brought into communion with one another and with God by grace. "Grace" simply means that God had called them into his presence as he calls us to share his life, through no deserving on man's part. Christians are not wiser or better looking or more holy than anyone else in the world. (Much evidence can be produced for that statement!) The difference is—we are "graced" people. "Grace" means that God has given us what an early Christian teacher called "a life in correspondence with God." Without this grace the first disciples would have been at loggerheads with one another, selfish and uncaring. But with this grace all their relationships with one another were transformed. Now they could witness to Christ's resur-

rection and lead a life which many people found a charming and
attractive thing (compare 2:47).

What Went Wrong? 5:1-11

The account of the young community described in 4:23-31 is
incomplete unless we look also at what went wrong in 5:1-11. It
is a terrible thing to discover sin—deceit, quarreling, argument, or
hatred—in a community of trust and love. But Acts is a very honest
book. It does not hide or gloss over the ugly aspects of the first
community of believers. We can see something of what went wrong
(and of why things still go wrong) in the strange story of Ananias
and Sapphira. Read it over and try to explain it in your own words.

One of the obvious truths to emerge from the passage is that
greed is always a problem. Luke wants us to understand the danger
of greed. Perhaps Ananias and Sapphira, who were quite well off,
disliked some of the rough and scrawny elements that had come
into the church. It was one thing to impress the apostle with the
promise of a generous gift. It was another to see their hard-earned
money being used for people not of their class or rank or education.

A profounder truth is to be seen: *lying destroys the community.*
The story raises a most acute problem in any community. When our
outward attitude bears no relation to what we feel or want inwardly,
we are really acting out a lie. We are hypocrites, pretending to be
what we are not. (The Greek word *hupocrites* means "actor.") We
are divided in ourselves. The lie is therefore a destructive thing: in
a marriage or a friendship it destroys trust. In fact, it will in the
end destroy the community itself. Peter's fierce words to Ananias
impress upon us the fact that lies are ultimately denials of God
(5:4).

FOR THOUGHT AND DISCUSSION

In the first passage that follows the writer speaks of the "Word,"
by which he means the essential content of the gospel.

The Word conquers time; it makes past and present contempo-
raneous. History beyond our reach here becomes history for us;

"formerly" becomes "now." An event in the inaccessible past is real presence; the pledge that sin is forgiven is no bare sign of a past event, but Calvary here present.

John S. Whale, *Christian Reunion: Historic Divisions Reconsidered*[3]

What do you think the writer means by saying that the Word of God "conquers time"? How does the Word of God come to you? What does it mean to say that the history of Jesus and of the first Christians becomes "history for us"? If Jesus is not "past Word" but "present Word" of God, what will this mean in your daily living?

The next passage raises the question of what it may have meant to share all things in common at Pentecost.

It is a plain fact that the more money a man has, the more temptations he has. There are a great many things which are no temptation to a poor man because they are impossible for him. He has no temptation to luxurious living. Caviare and champagne are no temptation to a man who has all he can do to get bread and butter. It is no temptation to a man to keep two homes when it takes him all his time to keep one. There is no temptation to idleness to a man who simply cannot afford to take a day off work. It is the simple fact that there are many more sins available to the man who has money in his pocket. The possession of money can be a real test of a man's moral fibre. To say that we "never had it so good" is also to say that we never had it so dangerous. The affluent society is also the society in peril.

William Barclay, *Ethics in a Permissive Society*[4]

Does this passage have any connection (as you see it) with Acts 4:32—35? Is there a distinctive witness for Christians in regard to money? Do you agree with the writer that "to have it made" is "to have it dangerous"? Do you think affluence is a danger? Why did the first Christians share all things? And (going back to the previous quotation) is this passage from Acts a "past Word" or a "present Word"?

Today, with the enormous amplification of news and of opinion, we are suffering from more than acceptable distortions of perspective. . . . In addition to the sheer volume of information there is the even more portentous fact of falsification and misinformation by which those in power are often completely intent not only on misleading others but even on convincing themselves that their own lies are historical truth.

Thomas Merton, "The Death of God and the End of History" [5]

In the light of this passage, comment on the effect of the lie in human communities—in the family, domestic or foreign affairs, or even in the church. How was the hypocrisy of Ananias and Sapphira an offense against God? against the church? Can you think of modern offenses parallel to theirs?

3

Advancing Beyond the Limits
Acts 6—8

A NEW STAGE in the development of the early church now begins. Three themes occupy our attention in this chapter: the
selection of seven men to serve the church; the heroic witness of one
of the seven, Stephen; and the spread of the gospel in Samaria.

SELECTING SEVEN MEN, 6:1–6

Apparently some time had elapsed between the end of chapter 5
of Acts and the beginning of chapter 6. The church had grown in
numbers, with Greek-speaking Jews (the "Hellenists") joining the
Aramaic-speaking community. Some widows among the Hellenists
had been neglected in the relief program. (Giving alms to the poor
was a practice highly esteemed by the early church.) The matter
came before the Twelve, who determined to appoint seven men
as their apostolic assistants.

Though they were not called "deacons," they had a service
which Luke calls *diakonia.* This service was defined as "serving
tables," i.e., taking care of the poor and administering the gifts of
the congregation. In contrast, the *diakonia* of the apostles was to
preach the word (6:4).

We make a mistake if we put a wedge between preaching the
word and serving the needy. The early church, as we have seen, ap-
plied the same word to both, and Jesus himself had said that the
Son of man came to serve, to act as deacon (Mark 10:45). The
assistance of the poor and needy was a duty that overshadowed all
others. The martyr bishop of Smyrna, Polycarp (died A.D. 155),

reminded his readers in a letter: "Let the presbyters also be compassionate, merciful to all, bringing back those that have wandered, caring for all the weak, neglecting neither widow, nor orphan, nor poor." In these words we find the characteristic spirit of early Christianity.

Can we not derive a number of insights from the above passage?

1) *New needs call for new ministries.* In a vivid phrase John A. T. Robinson says that true reformation will come when the church allows the forms of her life to grow around the shapes of the world's need. In your own opinion, how could the church dramatize what it means really to exist *for others?* What changes would this involve?

2) *Some of the conditions for a ministry of compassion can be listed.* A writer of the Middle Ages defined compassion as "finding your neighbor's mind in your own." To be compassionate is to respond imaginatively to the needs of the crippled, the wasted, the tormented, and the tired. In all of these we are to recognize Jesus' own scars. The seven to be chosen, according to the report, were to have the approval of the congregation, to be spiritually sensitive, and to have tact (6:3). An early writer commented wryly on this last point: "It needed very great superiority of mind to bear the complainings of the widows."

A Progress Report, 6:7

A brief report is now inserted informing us how the number of believers grew as a result of the preaching of the apostles. Zinzendorf, to whom the Moravians owe much of their renewal after the Thirty Years' War, used to wear a golden cross with an oval green front, in the center of which was a mustard tree. It was for him a symbol that even the least significant community of believers, like the grain of mustard seed, could grow to become—and Zinzendorf was the first to use the word—the ecumenical (worldwide) Christian church.

Stephen, 6:8—8:1

Stephen opened up a new era. The whole horizon now broadened immensely, but a hitherto unexperienced danger loomed up. As the Word was preached, resistance was intensified, and the church began to learn in experience what is involved in following Christ to the limit.

Stephen was one of the most important figures in Acts. He was the connecting link between Peter and Paul. He was among the first to glimpse the way in which the new gospel was bringing to fulfillment the faith of Israel. Unfortunately, we know very little about him. We can, however, learn certain things from the passage which we are studying.

1) *He was a man of broad vision and outlook.* He was a "Hellenist." In Jerusalem there were numbers of Jews who had been born and had grown up overseas in the so-called diaspora or dispersion. They spoke Greek and were familiar with Hellenistic culture. People like these generally were more international in their vision and attitudes than the Aramaic-speaking Jews of Judea.

2) *Stephen was faithful where he was.* We cannot speak about the "success of his long ministry"—he did not live to an honored old age. He sought only to be obedient to what God required of him. His obedience meant death. What will our obedience involve for us? God does not ask us to be successful, but faithful.

3) His brief ministry shows that *it is not the length but the quality of our service of the gospel that counts.* Stephen's whole ministry was confined to a very brief period. Sir Walter Scott quotes the saying in one of his novels: "One crowded hour of glorious life is worth an age without a name." That is amply illustrated here.

A theological student was killed in action in World War II, before he was even ordained. Yet to this day an annual award is made in his memory to the seminary student "whose fidelity to duty, love for others, and devotion to Jesus Christ are an abiding inspiration."[1] Stephen was a saint without glamour, but he is the more impressive as a model of all who are honored for their brief but thorough dedication to Christ.

4) *Opposition will arise when the full implications of the gospel are preached* (see especially 6:12–14). What Stephen wanted was to make of faith in Christ a truly worldwide faith, to break it out of its narrow confines. President James McCord of Princeton has said that religious people today can be divided into the "ecumenists" (those who stress the universal aspect of Christ's gospel) and the "tribalists" (those who narrow down its universal aspect). For Stephen the issue was basic: commitment to worldwide mission or limiting the gospel to one race. On this issue the gospel still stands or falls.

5) *Authentic preaching witnesses to the mighty acts of God.* It is unlikely that Stephen's sermon was actually preached as it stands. (See Appendix, p. 122.) But it was a unique, powerful, and strongly individual speech. Its theme was "the God of glory" (7:2). God is the one who makes himself known in the great events of Israel's history, and above all in Jesus.

The climax of the sermon was a denial of the charges made against him and a passionate appeal not to resist the Holy Spirit (7:51). Stephen called the councilors "stiff-necked" or stubborn. They had difficulty in moving from one position to another. They could not accept Stephen's understanding of the ways in which God acts. Until they could, they would remain bound to their narrow vision.

A thirteenth-century hymn of the Spirit says:

What is rigid gently bend;
What is frozen warmly tend;
Straighten what goes erringly.

We may be confident the Spirit is at work when stiff-necked, rigid, unbending people find themselves becoming gloriously free in the freedom of Christ.

6) *There is a witness to Christ that goes to the limit.* In the early church there was a threefold witness to Christ: in *word,* i.e., in preaching the resurrection; in *signs,* which are like sacraments of that word; and now for the first time in *suffering and death.*

In modern America no one is put to death on Christ's account, though at times in history to witness to Christ faithfully has in fact meant death. This was true often in the early church. To be a martyr was considered the most faithful kind of witness. Then, after the Roman state ceased to persecute Christians, the supreme witness was thought to be the monk. Who would you say represents a supreme witness to Christ in our day? What will total commitment to Christ involve for us?

Before his death Stephen made a very moving testimony: "I see the heavens opened, and the Son of man standing at the right hand of God." (7:56) Just for a moment he had seen something beyond description. His death was by stoning, which sounds as if he was lynched by a mob. One man in the vicinity was to be forever affected by his death—Saul. The dying words of Stephen must have struck his heart.

Begin

THE GOSPEL FOR SAMARIA, 8:1–25

1) *Violence* is like a deadly yeast that reproduces itself. On the very day of Stephen's death the assault on the church in Jerusalem grew more severe (8:1–3).

The people of God have always known violence like this. Do not fall into the trap of blaming the Jews for this crime. Violence is a human problem, not a Jewish or racial one. The people of God have suffered throughout history, and their pain has caused weeping from the beginning to the time of the concentration camps and since then. The ugliest things in our history, however, have been those times when we ourselves have been infected by the contagion of violence and have become the violent ones.

Saul's action (8:3) is of much interest to us. We know, of course, that Luke is preparing us for the great conversion of chapter 9, a story retold three times in Acts, and for the towering missionary achievements of this convert. But especially today it is his violence that captures our attention.

First, we see that *violence is in a sense the love that has gone wrong.* Even in its wrongness it still represents an affirmation of values. In "laying waste" the church, Saul was dominated by love— love for all that he valued. It was, of course, a distorted love. But even in the violence the love showed through. An expert who has studied human aggression tells us: "There is no love without aggression, but there is no hate without love . . . one can really hate only where one has loved and, even if one denies it, still does." [2] This means that there is always hope, even in a violent society, of channeling violence toward constructive ends. But that takes a revolution in thinking—a conversion in fact.

Second, *it is not the destructive act that is so wrong; it is the decision to act destructively.* In Goethe's play *Faust,* Mephistopheles, the evil one, demands of his victim that "he shall eat dust—and do so with pleasure." That is, he shall act like a beast and shall enjoy it. That is the real horror of destructive violence—not the act itself but the will to destroy and to like destroying. But the fact that violence is an act of will shows us also how to deal with the evil of acting destructively. It means that healing, to be most effective, is to be directed at the springs of our conduct. The gospel comes always to the heart.

2) *The fertile word.* In a sermon Leo the Great (c. 400–461) said: "By persecution the church is not made less, but rather made greater." The center of the apostolic gospel had so far been Jerusalem. Then despite—or because of—persecution, men and women who accepted the gospel of Christ and believed were scattered about. One of these was Philip, who after Stephen's death conducted an energetic ministry of evangelism and preaching in territory far beyond Jerusalem.

The churches we know are in little danger of persecution. For the most part they are (in Kipling's phrase) "nice and safe and out of the wet." Perhaps the persecution committed Christians will know today will be the threat of a growing, numbing indifference. If so, will it make us stronger and more resourceful, as it did the early church?

The first of two examples of a new breakthrough follows in 8:9–24, the second in 8:26–40. The gospel cannot be contained within any one caste, race, or community—it is for all the world, for half-caste Samaritan as well as Ethiopian eunuch.

3) *The Ethiopian eunuch.* There was no stopping Philip. The man who had broken through old traditions and restrictions to reach out into a new world in Samaria reached also into the life of an African official. The Ethiopian was not the first African to be brought to the presence of Jesus. As a baby Jesus had been carried into Egypt; and on the way to Calvary his cross had been carried by an African, Simon of Cyrene. Now an otherwise unknown man became the first in a long line that has stretched from him through Augustine to Chief Albert Luthuli and to the churches and believers of America who are part of the African tradition.

From the account we can learn two profound truths about the Christian faith. First, *there can never be barriers among those who have discovered what it means to belong to one another through "the good news of Jesus."* To raise divisions where Christ raised none is to deny that Christ breaks down the barriers that keep people apart (Eph. 2:14). Within the other, whether he or she is white or black, we are to learn to discover what Christ found so lovable that he died for it.

Second, *the ministry is an interpreting ministry.* The eunuch was familiar with the Jewish Scriptures and knew the picture of the suffering servant in Isaiah. Philip's work was to explain the good news of Jesus. The ministry opens up the inner meaning of the Word of God.

The story ends with an abrupt, almost violent separation (8:39). Perhaps the Ethiopian was in such a state of ecstasy that he was unaware of Philip's departure. There are some experiences in life so deeply moving that we are unaware of time, sense, sound, or sight while they last.

FOR THOUGHT AND DISCUSSION

The following passages may help us to clarify the meaning of what we have read—about new needs calling for new ministries; about total commitment to Christ; and about discovering what is lovable in the other.

Let us take a good look at the local Church and try to see what it might or should become. The local Church should become less of a structure with fixed membership and territorial boundaries and become more of a free floating redemptive process.

By "redemptive process" the writer means that the church is not to be thought of as a building or organization but as our whole daily life of involvement with other people, a life in which we grow toward the fullness of Christ. So she makes a distinction between what she calls the "institutional center" and "spontaneous communities" within an alive local church. The "center" is what we could call the congregation in its usual place of worship. The "spontaneous communities" might be, for instance, a peace fellowship group or a neighborhood group commissioned to work on public education, drug addiction, or youth ministry. At times such groups may want to celebrate the Lord's Supper together, and the writer says that anyone, whether the natural leader of the group or perhaps others, on a shifting basis, can exercise that ministry. She goes on:

This is much more the way the early church understood ministry. . . . Thus the terms "prophet," "teacher," "apostle" were not states of life, but functions corresponding to the work which the person, here and now, was being asked to fulfill for the community. In the same way the official ministry of local Churches, as well as more ephemeral roles, such as a leader of an addict center or even the leader of a summer work project, could be seen as kind of commissionings, and it would be well if we could use the rite of laying on of hands in this multi-functional way to

be a sign of these many ways in which the community sends
certain of its members forth to do particular tasks.

Rosemary Ruether, "Ministry in the Church of the Future" [3]

The writer's views on "church" and "ministry" are unusual and
some would say unorthodox. But do you think she helps you to understand Acts? How? How does what she says relate to your own study
group? What types of ministries needed in your community might
be approached by forming such action groups?

The second passage was written by a priest who suffered torture
in Brazil. What did he believe, and how did this affect his own life
and his attitude to his fellowmen? How would you compare him
to Stephen? His persecutors to Stephen's? Do these paragraphs say
anything to you of practical value regarding your commitment?

One day, during a pause in the interrogations and tortures, I
said that my work as a priest had consisted in living with the
people, working as a worker did; I only wanted to assist the
people in their struggle, be their friend. My torturers then beat
me more mercilessly and screamed at me: "False priest, traitor
of the people, of Brazil, of the church, of God, of Jesus Christ,
Communist priest. It's a sin for you to speak such rubbish, you
bastard of a priest!" . . .

We lived in a small cell, without adequate clothing or anything to cover ourselves with, eating always the same cold food
with small plastic forks and knives. We rarely got the chance
to shower or shave; there was one shower for fifty to seventy
prisoners. We were at the mercy of fleas, bedbugs and other in-
sects. Sometimes the slop-buckets of excrement would not be
taken away.

Six months without ever seeing the sun. Six months with a
bright light shining down all night long. Six months without any
news of people outside.

On every Saturday a list was taken of prisoners who wanted
to assist at Mass the following day. But we were never allowed
to have our names put on the list because we were being held

incommunicado. Nevertheless we celebrated the liberation of the whole people, we celebrated Easter, in our cells.

Antonio Albert Soligo, "Organized Torture in Brazil" [4]

The third passage is a moving account of how a black man had reduced himself to a cipher, to a being who was void of involvement with himself or the world. He felt threatened in his very being by a "beast" that was out to crush him. He turned "to the bottle, to the blade, to broads," but the beast was everywhere. His liberation began when he watched Malcolm X on television in the prison gymnasium.

Slowly I began to blink my eyes. More and more of his words filtered down to me via the black grapevines, words that substantiated that which I had always known. I existed, black and good. And love. He also gave the beast a name and told me of his nature, and that the beast could be conquered.

I opened my eyes and saw other black men speaking, teaching and singing with authority: John Coltrane, Leroi Jones, Archie Shepp, and others, going past the intellect, down to the root of Total Consciousness, down to a Love Supreme, down to pure sound, creating black images, and Love. I saw other black men of authority take to the pulpits and the streets and speak cf a God devoid of the beast. I saw Outer Authority being created that did not conflict with black Inner Authority. I saw Love. I saw that to love black is not to hate white, and is good. I saw space being created wherein I could stand straight. And I became whole. I stopped running from the beast and began to fight him.

Etheridge Knight, "On Being and Being Black" [5]

Does this sound to you like a "conversion"? What does the writer mean by "becoming whole"? In what way, if at all, can we help others be converted to Christ? What are you learning from Acts about evangelism? about world missions?

4

Lion of God

Acts 9

TAYLOR CALDWELL in a novel on the life of Paul calls him *Great Lion of God*. It is a majestic title. Paul had a lion's ferocity, courage, and pride. But we know also another Paul, the lamb from the lion, the prisoner of Christ from the persecutor of the people of God—as Augustine described him, "the enemy first, then the apostle."

PAUL'S THEOLOGY

Paul's faith and thinking both arose out of the vision of Christ that came on his approach to Damascus. There he recognized Jesus as the crucified and exalted Lord. No more decisive or influential encounter with Christ has ever occurred. Let us try to sum up very briefly the theology of Paul and see how at point after point it is related to the Damascus experience. It is no exaggeration to speak of him as the most creative thinker in the history of Christianity.

1) *Jesus Christ.* No one passage in the New Testament sums up more fully the meaning of Jesus Christ for Paul than the great hymn in Philippians 2:5–11. Read it over, and write down what you think are the major themes. Note what is stressed. First, *whatever God is, Jesus Christ is also.* He is "in the form of God," and has equality with God. Second, *in the incarnation he "emptied" himself.* This is a phrase difficult to explain in words. For the accomplishment of his mission the Son of God has taken the form of a servant and has been humbled to the depths of death itself. Third, *God has glorified*

him. Jesus is now the exalted Lord, worthy of being confessed by every tongue.

2) *The way of salvation*. Drawing on the language of the Old Testament and pouring new meanings into old ideas, Paul speaks in his Letters of why Jesus is central to faith and salvation. Jesus Christ died for the sinful. So central for human existence is this death that Paul makes it the constantly recurring theme of his preaching. This death has special significance for salvation. In Christ God has reconciled us to himself. By an almost indescribable love Christ has shared our human existence with us up to the climax of his death. His death frees us from the "curse of the law," from sin, from death, and from the powers of the present age (see Gal. 3:13; Rom. 5:16; 6:8). Jesus can therefore be called our peace, our *shalom*.

Paul "knew" Christ (as we might say) not so much with his head as with his heart. So great was the change from the-old-that-he-was to the-new-that-he-has-become that he speaks of the change as a new creation (as in 2 Cor. 5:17). The old Paul struggled with pride; he was totally convinced right was on his side. The new Paul discovered that all pride is broken in the cross. We have nothing of our own to boast of—neither goodness nor achievement nor even love. The only plea we can make is that Christ is our hope. And, as Paul knew well, to those who come empty-handed to God gifts are given beyond counting.

3) *Life in Christ*. The words "faith" and "believe" occur more frequently in Paul's writings than in any others in the New Testament; they especially abound in Romans and Galatians. Faith accepts and lays hold of God's action in Christ. For a full discussion of the idea, read Romans 10:4–17. Faith comes to birth in revelation, like the revelation on the road to Damascus. But preaching the gospel is itself part of revelation, and faith also comes from what is preached about Christ.

What does faith believe? It believes, like ancient Abraham, that even a body that has no life in it is able to live and be fruitful (Rom. 4:16–25). God is the God who gives life to the dead, and he raised Jesus from the dead in a fruitful way—"for our justification."

To believe that the death of Jesus is the means of life is to confess that Jesus is Lord. Faith is thus the first step in a new existence called life in Christ.

4) *The church.* Because of Jesus Christ a new creation, a new possibility, has come about in the world. For the first Christians baptism was a sign of death and resurrection: it was a sign of the drowning of our old selves and of being lifted up into the new life. So baptism affirms that those who hitherto have been divided have "put on" Christ, so that they are one new being in him. The new life is really new, for the Spirit of Christ dwells in the believer. To be baptized is to be publicly identified with Jesus Christ—in baptism we are crucified with him, buried with him, and restored to life with him (Col. 2:12-14).

To belong to the community of this new life is the same thing for Paul as to be "in Christ" or "in the church." For the church is the beginning of a redeemed human race. In this new community all are one in Christ—Jew and Greek, slave and free, male and female (Gal. 3:28).

The most important ministry of this community is preaching, which exalts the God who sets men and women free and through which faith is begotten; baptism, through which the relationship to Christ and to the community is signified and sealed; and the Lord's Supper, through which the community experiences at the deepest level its unity with Christ, and in which the many who share the bread become one. The church's concerns are therefore always concerns of liberation, newness, and all that has to do with the human race.

THE ROAD TO DAMASCUS, 9:1-19

Saul, the young man who had been officially involved in the lynching of Stephen, was a Hellenist from Tarsus and an intensely loyal Jew. He hated men like Stephen and others who belonged to "the Way," because he thought their new faith dishonored the sacred law. So he had broken into homes seeking those who shared the views of the martyr Stephen, though many fled Jerusalem and so were able to escape him (8:1–3).

Some of these had apparently made their way to Damascus. To this city therefore Saul turned, "still breathing threats and murder." He had in his possession letters from the supreme council in Jerusalem allowing him to bring the followers of the Way back to Jerusalem for trial. (The journey is about one hundred and fifty miles. A man who travels that distance by foot or on an ass must be deadly serious about his purpose.)

Traveling as he probably did through Galilee, Saul passed through the country in which Jesus himself had preached two or three years earlier. On the approach to Damascus he had a vision of flashing light, the shock of which felled him, and he heard a voice: "Saul, why do you persecute me?" The risen Christ and his violent opponent had met. Dazed, blinded, and confused, Saul had to be led to the city by those who accompanied him.

1) *The meaning of Paul's conversion.* What happened on the road to Damascus? Paul was a man of massive energy and of gigantic intellect, but also of compassion. Perhaps he had repressed the serious doubts that his sensitive spirit felt concerning his part in the earlier violence. It is right to ask questions about the psychology or background of the Damascus experience.

Paul himself was convinced that he had received a resurrection appearance of the Son of God. In many of his later writings we catch a memory of the momentous happening: "Have I not seen Jesus our Lord?" (1 Cor. 9:1) God "was pleased to reveal his Son to me." (Gal. 1:16) In a curious phrase in one of his Letters he speaks about having been "caught up to the third heaven." (2 Cor. 12:2) If this refers to his conversion, the experience on the Damascus road had given him a sensation of being totally lifted out of himself to a new level of reality. So we properly speak of what happened on the Damascus road as a conversion, because there was a complete reversal of what he was. Paul had passed the first crucial point in becoming the apostle of the Gentiles.

His world had been overturned—as a man, as a believer, and as an agent of the authorities. In his disarray he was brought "by the

hand" to Damascus (9:8; contrast this with the hand that was ready
to murder in 9:1). He was weak and humbled, but also he had
learned a lesson that he never afterward forgot—God's grace came
to him at his weakest moment; God's power is at its best in weakness
(2 Cor. 12:9). He could never later have preached how Christ
humbled himself to accept death without that personal humbling
before Damascus. Somehow we don't think of the "new" Paul as
more remote from us, but actually as closer to us—more human,
more vulnerable, more loving. He seems to say to us: "if God can
use me with all my frailties, don't ever doubt that he can use you
also!"

So Paul's conversion meant a humbling. But it also meant more.
In an unforgettable sentence St. John Chrysostom once said: "The
chief danger consists not so much in falling when fighting but in
remaining upon the ground after the fall." Something very revealing
about conversion and the Christian life is described in 9:10–19. Paul
had fallen. But he was also lifted up. From the mouth of a man who
might well have regarded him as a devil Saul heard the greeting,
"Brother!" The speaker who said this was a believer called Ananias.
He could have learned to say it only in a new kind of community
in which people call one another "brother," "sister," and "friend."
So *to become a member of this community means to be brought out
of the closed circle of our own world into a society of friends.*

2) *The conversion gave Paul his message.* Ananias had learned
in a mysterious way (9:15) that the broken figure before him was
to bring God's name before men. The message of Paul the apostle
came to him first on the road to Damascus, even though it took him
years to learn its full meaning. It was the message of Easter and of
faith.

Paul learned on the way to Damascus, first, that Christ was risen
and, second, that the old ways of coming into fellowship with God
had broken down. They had failed because by them "none is righteous." But a new era had dawned: faith has come, and we are
made right with God by faith (Gal. 3:24–25).

3) *The conversion gave Paul his ministry.* In one account of his

conversion Paul reported that he had heard the words, "Saul, Saul, it hurts you to kick against the goads." (26:14) The reference almost seems to fit Paul's future more than his past. It was as though Jesus were saying to him: from now on you are at my service, and I will give you no release from it. From the time of Damascus Paul was Christ's man.

FOR THOUGHT AND DISCUSSION

The first passage which follows raises the question of whether Paul's conversion should be a model of all conversions. The writer seems to say "no" *and* "yes." How do you reconcile what he says?

> For years I asked all young communicants whether they would describe themselves as those who had found Christ and knew Him as Saviour in the fullest converted sense, or whether they would call themselves seekers and disciples, prepared to pledge themselves in loyalty to follow Jesus wherever He led them. And, looking back, I cannot say that those who with assurance and sometimes complacency said they had found Christ and been saved with a full experience of redemption afterwards always made good as Church members; rather I would say that very often those who came less confidently as seekers went farther and did better in the end.

Does your experience agree with his? In which category were you when you made your profession of faith? In which are you now?

But perhaps the real sin against the Holy Spirit, the writer adds, is to say that Pentecost is not for everybody:

> The status of discipleship without a baptism of the Holy Spirit is a precarious and provisional one, full of disappointments and frustrations, as those men at Ephesus [Acts 19:1–7] knew well. The fact that most of the people in our Churches are still there and have not been led to expect anything further is precisely what is wrong with the church today.

W. R. Forrester, *Conversion*[1]

How accurate is this analysis? If it is true, what can be done about it? What can you do about it?

The second passage, also dealing with a kind of conversion, recounts an episode from World War II.

My conscience seems to become little by little sooted. . . . If I can soon get out of this war and back on the soil where the clean earth will wash away these stains! I have also other things on my conscience. . . . A man named H., accused of being the local Gestapo agent in one small town, was an old man of seventy. His wife and he looked frightened and old and miserable. . . . I was quite harsh to him and remember threatening him with an investigation when I put him under house arrest. . . . Day before yesterday word came that he and his wife had commited suicide by taking poison. Fain and I went back and found them dead in their beds, he lying on his back and reminding me, gruesomely enough, of my father, she twisted over on her side with her face concealed. At the bedside was a card on which he had scrawled: "Wir mussten elend zu Grunde gehen. Der Herr Gott verzeihe uns. Wir haben niemandem leid getan". . . . We must perish miserably. God forgive us. We have done no one any harm. The incident affected me strongly and still does. I was directly or indirectly the cause of their death. . . . I hope it will not rest too hard on my conscience, and yet if it does not I shall be disturbed also.

J. Glenn Gray, *The Warriors*[2]

Does this in any way help to explain Paul's conversion? What are some of the factors involved in any massive change of outlook and life?

The third passage is a kind of meditation, written by a man who was immersed in international politics. But it sheds some light on the meaning of Paul's Damascus experience.

I came to a time and place where I realized that the Way leads to a triumph which is a catastrophe, and to a catastrophe which is a triumph, that the price for committing one's life would be reproach, and that the only elevation possible to man lies in the depths of humiliation. After that, the word "courage" lost its meaning, since nothing could be taken from me.

Dag Hammarskjöld, *Markings*[3]

Paul often speaks of suffering. Read, for example, 2 Corinthians 4:7–11 and compare what he says with this passage. What was the triumph that was a catastrophe for Paul? In your own words, what does Hammarskjöld mean by saying that the only elevation possible to us lies in the depths of humiliation? What does Paul mean by saying that we carry with us in our body the death of Jesus?

Open Doors and Crumbling Walls

Acts 10:1—11:26

O N A WINDY DAY on Main Street in a southern city, a white lady lost her tight-fitting hat. A Negro truck driver stopped, retrieved and returned the hat, and quickly drove away. The grateful shopper wrote a warm letter of thanks to the morning paper, praising the trucker's "unadulterated kindness."

For most of us public goodwill is easy. Would the same appreciative lady have been willing to welcome the trucker if he and his family moved into the house next door? It is at this point—where we live, eat, swim, play, and worship—that most of us have to face the difficulty of helping to pull down walls.

It seems second nature to build walls to keep ourselves apart from people not of our kind. Yet the words of Robert Frost from "Mending Wall" may tell us more about a better nature: "Something there is that doesn't love a wall." The passage which follows tells us of a crisis in the early days of the church, when a very complex and hard decision was made about tearing down walls.

THE WALLS COME TUMBLING DOWN, 10:1–48

In Caesarea a Roman officer called Cornelius had attached himself with his family to the synagogue. He was an Italian and a pagan. Synagogues in the Gentile world often had adherents of this kind, who were sometimes called "God-fearers." (See Acts 13:16, for example.) They obeyed the teachings of the Jews and with them worshiped the one God, though they had not received circumcision and did not observe the full requirements of the Jewish law.

Cornelius was one of these devout, generous, and spiritual men. It had come to him in a vision that he should invite Simon Peter to his house. But it was prohibited by law and custom for a Jew like Peter to eat and drink with a Gentile. Since Gentiles did not observe Jewish law regarding foods that were clean and unclean, a loyal Jew could not have a meal with a man like Cornelius. The wall of division was unyielding.

Then, in one of those marvelous coincidences of life—which the early Christians did not hesitate to call visions, though such language is more difficult to us—it came to Peter that he should resist every inborn instinct and call nothing unclean that God has cleansed (10:9–16). He became utterly convinced by God's Spirit that the meaning of his dream was that God shows no partiality (10:34). At this moment Peter's eyes were opened; he saw a whole world waiting for the good news of peace by Jesus Christ (10:35).

As soon as Peter made this breakthrough into a new way of thinking, there was an astonishing demonstration of the power of the Spirit—it was like a new Pentecost (10:44–48). Peter's words were the great liberating Magna Carta of the early church. A recent writer has a beautiful and simple verdict on Peter's decision: "he accepted their hospitality; he ate and drank with them; a new church was born." [1]

There are many ways of learning about ourselves from this story. There is, first, a personal meaning.

1) *Christ calls us to become truly "freed up" people.* In what many regard as his best work Luther wrote about what he called "two propositions concerning the freedom and the bondage of the spirit." The two are these: "A Christian is a perfectly free lord of all, subject to none. A Christian is a perfectly dutiful servant of all, subject to all." [2] In the balanced tension between these two ideas— freedom and service—we can discover the meaning of the Christian life.

Peter's attitude to those not of his race was deep-rooted. An outlook that has been solidified from youth cannot easily be altered overnight. It was second nature to him to draw a line between those who belonged to the covenant community and those who did not.

He couldn't associate with those who, he had been taught to believe, had no part in his community. So he built a wall to separate himself from "unclean" pagans. He was not free.

As he had done before, he impulsively objected to what Jesus asked (10:14). He still was (in a deep sense) the same "old" Peter. He had still to think his way into the fully "new" Peter, the Peter who would show no partiality because Christ wanted all bad walls of division to be pulled down. As long as he was the same old Peter he was not free of prejudice. He had a limited view of the covenant community.

When he became "freed up," he was no longer in bonds, the bonds of an old, restrictive, narrow outlook. But this freedom meant not only being "free from," it also meant being "free to"—free to welcome a stranger as a brother whom he now loved and served for the sake of the gospel.

There is a second insight in the passage.

2) *It is a genuinely liberating thing to discover our oneness with others.* Peter's discovery was that the family of faith does not draw lines to exclude outsiders, for all alike share in the call of God. The love that binds people in the unity of the Spirit is an open love that creates a true brotherhood. In it all the old barriers of age, social rank, or sex have been declared nonessential. All are the same in the sight of God. To raise these fundamental barriers in a divisive way is to go back to the old ways from which Christ seeks to free us.

To discover that the church is this kind of *new* community is a liberating experience. Look carefully at the words in 10:27, "he went in." With that step Peter entered a different world. He was never quite the same after this. He still faltered and made mistakes, but on the basic question he was now committed. In a book written over a hundred years ago in Scotland, the author, persecuted for his own beliefs, sums up well this liberating discovery: "If we refuse to be in Christ the brothers of men, we cannot be in Christ the sons of God."

A third insight emerges from the story.

3) *New experiences force us to deepen our theology.* The en-

counter with Cornelius deepened Peter's whole thinking about God. God is the God of every nation (10:35). Jesus is not only "Lord and Christ," as Peter had said earlier (2:36), using characteristically Jewish titles; he is "Lord of all," Lord of Gentile and Jew alike (10:36).

The human family is shaken and frightened today by many problems: our abuse of the earth, the squandering of human resources on war, the difficulty of living together with those who belong to different races, the generation gap. All of these problems of the family of man will affect the words and actions by which we try today to express our faith in Christ, the Lord of all.

CRITICS OF THE NEW FREEDOM, 11:1–18

Not surprisingly, the initiative of Peter was quickly criticized. New initiatives in the life of the church, and especially dramatic departures from custom, often provoke surprise, offense, or resentment. The issue naturally comes to a head in theology. So from the first we find serious theological dispute within the Christian community.

The issue which divided Peter and the circumcision party was not that he had baptized Cornelius (10:48), but that he had gone into the centurion's house and eaten with him (11:3). It is illuminating for us today to see how the early church dealt with an urgent issue over which a split was quite likely to occur. Three things, each instructive for us, can be discerned in the passage.

1) *Facing the problem.* The first thing to note is that they faced the disputed question openly. Those who disagreed with one another disclosed their honest and firmly held convictions; they did not mask them. The profoundest kind of human conversation is one where spiritual convictions confront one another. The passage presents us with two quite different understandings of faith and life. Note the position taken by Peter.

2) *Stating the facts.* Peter openly stated the facts as he saw them. The basis of any human relationship is honesty in saying what we

have done and why. Peter did not apologize for what he had done, or play it down. He said straightforwardly what had happened. By the time he came to describe the activity of the Spirit among the uncircumcised, his critics had nothing left to say. Peter's final question could not be debated: "Who was I that I could withstand God?"

3) *Agreeing to live together, even with tensions.* Lastly, even though the two parties were divided from each other, they knew it was better to live together in a tension that might very well prove to be a creative one, provided there was sufficient love and respect. It was as if the apostles and the brothers in Judea said to Peter: the matter in dispute is still unresolved. But in a way we do not understand, God is clearly at work. Let us stay together and give glory to God for the good that is done!

Thus the passage ends with a doxology. A new and liberating discovery had been made: God wills life even for the Gentiles, and this life comes through the repentance that is prompted by the proclamation of the gospel.

In the contemporary church, tension and division are common. There is much talk about a split between the conservatives and the liberals. We need to learn more from the first Christians: it is better to face openly what divides us than to divide; it takes wisdom to enter into the deeply held convictions of the other; and it makes good sense to say that we are incomplete without one another. If we can do and say these things, it should not surprise us that God will continue to do great things among us.

THE FOUNDATION OF THE GREAT
MISSIONARY CHURCH AT ANTIOCH, 11:19–26

The first preaching of the apostles on the day of Pentecost started a chain reaction. The Christian mission began to expand through Jews who had come to Jerusalem for the feast (2:8–11). It burst out again in Philip's preaching in Samaria (8:5) and perhaps through the influence of his Ethiopian convert (8:26–40). It came to a climax in the conversion of the pagan Cornelius and the baptism of many Gentiles (ch. 10). Now Luke reports that large numbers were converted at Antioch.

After the death of Stephen, Greek-speaking believers had been scattered (8:4). Eventually some of them had come to Antioch, the third largest city in the Roman Empire, home to Syrians, Jews, Greeks, and Romans. It was an open city, notorious for its decadence and for its love of witty epigrams and nicknames. If the gospel could take root here, no community is too hard a soil for it!

In Antioch the disciples of Jesus were first named "Christians." In the Jewish world of thought a name was a very powerful thing. To pronounce someone's name meant to make him present in some way. So when God's name is pronounced, it must be uttered with reverence, because he is holy—"Our Father in heaven, may your name be held holy." To hold God's name holy means to worship him—by our lips and in our lives; it means to remember that we are his and that we are to show something of his own character in our lives.

To be named "Christian," therefore, means more than to belong to the community which calls on the name of Jesus (1 Cor. 1:2). It also means to be Christ's own, to live as in his presence, to recognize his demands, to struggle with his claims upon us, to enjoy his gifts, to love our neighbor for his sake.

FOR THOUGHT AND DISCUSSION

In the first of the passages which follow, the theme brings us back to the story of Peter and Cornelius. In a modern form we struggle with the dilemma and its resolution which are at the heart of that episode.

In the plainest and simplest of terms, what is already taking place in the black ghetto must also take place in the church and in the white community: REBELLION! Theologically necessitated rebellion against all that imprisons us and keeps us from acting as responsible children of God. We must rebel against our fear, rebel against our neurotic needs to oppress. We must rebel against the systems and structures in the church and society that foster, support and perpetuate racism. We must rebel against programs, ostensibly designed to assist the downtrodden, which in reality result in the hindrance of change. We must rebel against a racist culture that inculcates prejudice and hatred on every level of consciousness. We must rebel against all that holds us powerless to act in love and justice toward our fellowman. . . .

A call to rebellion may sound a bit frightening, but it is precisely what the gospel of Jesus Christ has always been. And our teacher and example in the art of rebelling is none other than our Lord himself. His life and ministry, his teaching and his command direct us to defy and destroy the evil powers that seek to take away our freedom and render us powerless to love effectively and justly.

Joseph R. Barndt, *Why Black Power?*[3]

Do you agree that the gospel is a call to rebellion in the sense understood by the author? If the church did move in the direction to which he calls it, would this help us to understand the experience of being one under God in Jesus Christ? How did the words "black ghetto," "racism," and "black power" affect your attitude toward this quotation? What can you learn from this experience?

In the second passage we consider our freedom in the gospel.

We are always . . . commanded to act lovingly, but how to do it depends on our own *responsible* estimate of the situation. Only love is a constant; everything else is a variable. The shift to relativism carries contemporary Christians away from code ethics, away from stern iron-bound do's and don'ts, away from prescribed conduct and legalistic morality.

. . . [Love] is the *only* principle that always obliges us in conscience. Unlike all other principles you might mention, love alone when well served is always good and right in every situation. Love is the only universal. But love is not something we *have* or *are,* it is something we *do.* Our task is to act so that more good (i.e., loving-kindness) will occur than any possible alternatives; we are to be "optimific," to seek an optimum of loving-kindness. It is an attitude, a disposition, a leaning, a preference, a purpose.

Joseph Fletcher, *Situation Ethics*[4]

This passage is often regarded as one of the first statements of the so-called new morality. In what ways are you critical of it? In what ways do you find it helpful in trying to understand Peter's breakthrough from a restrictive to an open outlook? in trying to understand your own relationship to others?

In the third passage we ask questions about the meaning of "the open church." The writer says that when a break of communication occurs in a community, people stop talking. Later it becomes possible to respect one another at a distance. But time eventually does its work and a deeper kind of conversation becomes possible.

Experience also shows that when dialogue is initiated the discussion may set itself three main kinds of objectives. The first seeks to remove more or less grave matters in disputes still outstanding on either side. This can lead to determining more clearly the conditions of harmonious common life. The second kind involves defining in common those domains in which interests are found to coincide and which are sufficiently independent of differences of conviction to make common action possible (and sometimes indispensable) once the principles of acceptable relations between the parties have been properly established. Finally, the third kind of objective concerns an abiding human possibility which may very well be realized: each may bring to the other new resources of vitality and progress even on the plane of the convictions in which they differ.

Dominique Dubarle, "Dialogue and Its Philosophy" [5]

Does this throw any light on the relationship of Peter to the apostles and brothers in Judea? How should we Christians deal with those from whom we are separated by deep convictions?

6

On to the Bound of the Waste
Acts 12:24—14:28

T HE SCENE IS SET in 12:24–25 for the account of the commis-
sioning of Barnabas and Paul for their new work. The com-
parative peace which followed the death of Herod Agrippa had
given time for growth in the church. John Mark, the cousin of
Barnabas, is introduced to us. The first missionary journey is about
to begin.

A NEW ENTERPRISE IS UNDERTAKEN, 13:1–3

Some leaders of the church in Antioch felt led by the voice of
the Spirit to select two men for the task of proclaiming the gospel
and establishing Christian communities in ways as yet untried. At
the meeting there were present, besides Barnabas and Paul, some
prophets (preachers—1 Cor. 14:3), some teachers, and three others
of whom we know nothing—Symeon (whose name suggests an
African origin), Lucius of Cyrene (who possibly may be Luke himself), and Manaen (an official of high rank).

The brief description is of much interest to us because it gives us
a little light on two subjects about which scholars are very much in
the dark: worship and ministry in the early church.

1) *A glimpse at worship in the early church.* We do not know
but it is a fair guess that the worship spoken of here was the "breaking of bread" of which we have read earlier (2:42). When we see
the apostles gathered together after the resurrection of Jesus, we
realize that it was characteristically a common meal that brought

them together. With the common meal there was combined from the beginning the memorial meal of the Lord, or the Lord's Supper as we often call it. Later, apparently, the two acts were separated, the common meal being held in the evening and the meal of the Lord, or eucharist, held in the early morning.

Another practice of the early church is mentioned here, fasting. In Old Testament days fasting was part of the worship of Yahweh. In the Prophets it was an outward expression of a radical turning toward God and the love of one's neighbor (Isa. 58:3–8). Jesus himself began his public ministry with a fast in the desert, and he clearly valued fasting as an expression of an attitude which he honored (see Matt. 4:1–2; 6:17).

2) *A solemn act of setting apart.* The passage also tells us of the setting apart of Barnabas and Paul by the prophets and teachers. Henceforth they were to fulfill the apostolic task of bearing witness to the resurrection and building up the church. Their new ministry would make them wanderers over the face of the Empire. They were to be vagabonds for the sake of the gospel. Paul could never have forgotten the solemn act. He used the same language of being "set apart" or "specially chosen" in Romans 1:1 and Galatians 1:15.

3) *Insights into the church's life.* In these brief glimpses into the life of the early church certain points stand out.

First, *in the truly alive church the initiative lies with the Spirit.* The risen Lord has his purpose for us before we ever respond to his action. At times we think of the church as a vast machine which depends on us for its functioning. In contrast, the early church was constantly aware that the Spirit was at work opening up new paths, calling individuals into service, enlarging horizons.

Second, *in the central activity of worship the people of God come to understand more clearly what it means to be the people of God.* In worship we become more and more fully what we already are, the people of God. We enter into the whole process of salvation which began with Good Friday and Easter and will continue till the end of time.

Third, *the church is the sphere in which we learn to feel and also to express love and concern for our neighbor.* There is always the danger that worship may insulate us from human beings in their need, rather than open our eyes to them. All true worship forces us in the end into costly involvement in the world; translated into the common currency of daily life, that may mean work in community councils, political parties, or agencies of social concern. This is something of the idea suggested by "fasting" in the passage. Isaiah long ago saw the connection between worship and conduct. "What is the fast and the day acceptable to the Lord?" he asks. "Is not this the fast . . . to loose the bonds of wickedness, to undo the thongs of the yoke, to let the oppressed go free?" (Isa. 58:6) In fact fasting, properly understood, may be a helpful way of showing that, whatever may be our own just claims, we and our property are at the disposal of our neighbors.

Fourth, *the church is always to be conscious of a waiting world.* The Christians at Antioch remembered the words of Jesus: "make disciples of all nations." And this involves not simply declaring but expressing in acts of compassion the love of Christ for the entire human race.

The Mission of Barnabas, Paul, and John Mark, 13:4—14:28

The horizon was now expanded in the apostolic mission. There had been missionary activity before among the Gentiles; now it became a plan and a policy. There had been travel to the west before; now the whole center of gravity was shifted westward.

The three who were sent out by the church at Antioch made their way to Cyprus, the home of Barnabas. It was a rich island— its name means "copper," and its copper mines had been exploited over the centuries. Many Jews lived there, drawn by the copper business. In their synagogue the three found a place to proclaim their gospel.

1) *A clash between two world views.* Ninety miles to the west lay the port town of Paphos, with a famous temple of Aphrodite. In

the court of the Roman proconsul a dramatic episode occurred. The proconsul, Sergius Paulus, had become interested in the message of the apostles. But he was under the influence of Elymas, a weird Svengali-like figure who probably realized that his prestige as a magician was being undermined by Barnabas and Paul. Like a ferocious Old Testament prophet, Paul exposed the sham of Elymas. Luke records that Elymas was blinded. By invoking the name of Jesus the apostle called into operation the power and authority of the Lord. The consul was filled with a deep sense of wonder and became a believer. We do not know what the magic was that Paul condemned, but there *are* ways of life that cannot coexist with Christianity. Think of those who exploit others. Think of those who try to manipulate people. Think of the mass suggestion of much advertising and propaganda. The last thing this kind of "magic" wants is real freedom for the people. It wants to control and direct the minds and lives of others.

In your own view, what are some ways of life so opposed to the "better way" of Christian love that they cannot coexist with Christianity? On what grounds would you judge them to be impossible for a Christian to embrace? The greatest gift that Paul had to offer, and it still comes to us in the gospel and the abundant life which Christ bestows, was the grace that frees people for self-criticism, for a better way of living, and for respect of all human personality.

2) *Mountains and a waste of seas.* The description of 13:13–14 is so sketchy that we have little idea of the sheer harshness of the journey. From Paphos to Pisidian Antioch, Paul and Barnabas had to take ship over treacherous waters; they had to breathe the dangerous swamp mists of the coastland; and they had to climb nearly four thousand feet to Pisidian Antioch. They had no protection from pirates and no bridges over rivers. The apostles knew what their obedience cost. But now the heartland of Asia Minor was opened up to the gospel of Christ.

3) *Proclaiming the story of salvation.* Lodgings for the travelers were found in Pisidian Antioch, probably among Jews, and on the Sabbath they attended the synagogue. After the reading of Scripture

the two visitors were asked if they wanted to speak. Paul grasped the opportunity, and what follows in 13:15–41 is a typical example of missionary preaching. Read the sermon and note its content and character as Paul traces the story of salvation from the exodus to the resurrection.

True preaching always has an effect, hidden or public. The Word of God is an active word. It sets a choice before us. Many who heard Paul embraced his teaching. On them he urged faithfulness to the grace he had proclaimed. The next Sabbath even larger crowds assembled (13:44). But by this time opposition was mounting. What accounts for the rising hostility? (See 13:45.)

It was soon clear that no fruits could grow in this sterile soil. So Paul and Barnabas took a momentous step: "we turn to the Gentiles." (13:46) Christ is to be proclaimed as the light of the nations. The decision tells us something important about failure. Paul and Barnabas had failed to do what they set out to do. But it is not our failure, it is what we do with it, how we respond to it, that counts. From almost any standpoint the cross of Calvary was a bitter, painful failure. Perhaps those who experience the "lesser Calvaries" of their own failures are closer to the "unsuccessful" God of Good Friday. Failure has been called a sacrament. It can be a means of grace. Because of the failure at Antioch there was a dramatic shift in the Christian mission, and a whole new world was opened up.

4) *A healing and a rescue.* In one of the cities to which the apostles came a cripple in the audience heard Paul speak about faith. The impact of the right word to a man who was hungry for that gift was immense. He started to walk (14:8–18). The sight so impressed the crowds that they concluded Paul and Barnabas were gods come to earth. Indeed, they all but offered sacrifice to the horrified apostles.

The passage is helpful in disclosing to us some clues to what is involved in teaching or proclaiming the Christian message.

There is, first, *identification:* "we are like you." (14:15) There is no place for "before" or "after," "superior" or "inferior" in the Christian community. T. E. Lawrence ("Lawrence of Arabia") describes a lesson in leadership which he learned from the Arabs: "Every enrolled man should serve in the line of battle."[1] In a similar way the apostle identifies himself with those he lives among. A letter written by Dietrich Bonhoeffer when he was in the United States in the summer of 1939 expresses the same idea: "I must live through this difficult period of our national history with the Christian people of Germany. I will have no right to participate in the reconstruction of Christian life in Germany after the war if I do not share the trials of this time with my people."[2]

The passage tells us something also about *the point of contact* which the teacher tries to make. Paul began by speaking about something the countryfolk would know of—rain, the seasons, and the harvest on which their lives depended (14:17). Not all missionaries have had the apostle's skill in getting across to an audience. Sometime ago at a mission service in a mining town the missioner—a professor of theology who obviously did not know any better—opened his first sermon by saying, "There's too much ego in the cosmos." He lost his audience in the first five seconds!

Notice, thirdly, *the appeal for commitment*. The apostle sought always a commitment, a turning to the living God and Father of Jesus Christ (14:15). When we really "hear" the Word of God, we shall be forced at times to turn away from one way of living and to embrace a better way.

The visit to Lystra came to an abrupt end with the appearance of hostile elements from two of the places visited by the apostles earlier. The crowd was quickly turned against the apostle whom they had so recently hailed as the spokesman of the gods. Nearly dead, Paul was dragged from the city. But his body withstood the ferocious punishment, and indeed the next day he was able to resume his travels (14:19–20).

5) *Journey home.* If you look at the map (p. 6) you will see that Paul's journey home lay directly eastward over the Taurus Mountains. He chose not to go that way, however, and instead turned back westward—to the very dangers he had recently escaped. But he wanted to strengthen and organize the communities of faith which he had helped to establish.

Finally they returned to Antioch, whence they had first set out. Here they celebrated the results of their mission. God had been and was to be proclaimed as accessible to all, not through the old ways but through the way of faith in the promises and acts of God.

FOR THOUGHT AND DISCUSSION

What we have learned in this chapter will help us as we consider three critical questions: Can we experience the Holy Spirit as vividly as did the earliest Christians? Where do we see the Spirit at work today? Are there ways of life wholly opposed to the gospel?

A man may come to seek baptism in the Holy Spirit because he has seen and believed the work of the Spirit in the life of a friend. He then trusts Jesus in prayer and expects that the Lord will renew in him the gifts and fruits bestowed in baptism but not fully activated in a living way. In the answer to that prayer, Jesus often becomes more real to the believer. He is much closer, more present in one's life. He is not only at the right hand of the Father; he the risen Lord is really alive among the members of his body. This old belief becomes a new awareness, becomes really real to the believer. The relationship in faith between this man and the Father through Christ has been deepened, transformed, and has become the center of personal existence. It would be false to characterize this new-found faith-life as a purely emotional experience. Certainly human emotion is involved in any act of love, and people respond emotionally according to their temperament. But it seems better to speak of this new faith on the level of a penetration and all-encompassing awareness and conviction which involves the whole body-person with all of his human qualities in a response of deep commitment.

Kevin and Dorothy Ranaghan, *As the Spirit Leads Us* [3]

What do you think the writers mean by the "new awareness" that becomes "really real"? What had been lacking in the "old belief"? Does the experience they describe seem real to you? How would you describe verbally (or through some other medium) your experience of Christ and of the Spirit?

The second question deals also with the doctrine of the Spirit. A task force of church members met within recent years to discuss the doctrine and came to the conclusion that the Spirit is at work in at least these areas of their personal observation:

Areas of reconciliation
>   The ecumenical movement
>   The United Nations
>   Labor-management relations
>   Councils of the church

Areas of tension
>   The East-West conflict
>   Racial problems and demonstrations for human rights
>   Economic problems and their resolutions
>   Abolition of capital punishment

Areas of personal concern
>   Alcoholics Anonymous
>   Medicare
>   Natural or human disasters that bring about sincere efforts to eliminate such disasters
>   Mission work of the church in preaching, teaching, and healing.[4]

Would you agree that it is hard to distinguish between the work of the Spirit and serious humanitarian concerns of cultural and social movements of our time which involve secular world views? How does the Spirit's work in conversion differ from his work in social movements, if it does?

The last quotation deals with the problem of violence.

Kids in the balcony at a recent Times Square showing of "Dirty Harry" were stomping their feet with glee at each shooting or beating. One boy was coming on strong as a munitions expert, giving his girl a run-down on the range and impact of each weapon as it appeared. When the massacres ended and the

house lights came up, he breathed a sigh of deep satisfaction and
said quietly: "That was nice."

Joseph Morgenstern, "The New Violence" [5]

Is the new violence of TV and movies opposed to the gospel?
Where do you draw the line? Is all violence opposed to the gospel?
What are the restraints against violence in your own life? Are these
external or internal? If you think that a certain way of living is
impossible for a Christian, what is it, and what are the factors involved in your judgment?

Westward Ho!

Acts 15:36—17:34

It was said of Napoleon, "He has his mind on the future." That was even more true of Paul. On his first missionary journey he had caught a glimpse of a whole world brought into allegiance to Christ.

A Quarrel and a Realignment, 15:36–41

The necessary business at Jerusalem had been settled. Now Paul was restless and felt drawn to go back from Antioch to the apostolic work which he had begun earlier. Perhaps he feared that the faith of the young churches was wavering.

His friend Barnabas wanted to take John Mark, but Paul was not in favor of taking a man who, he thought, had deserted them in a crucial situation earlier (13:13). With complete honesty Luke admits that there was a violent quarrel. It was resolved by a realignment of the apostolic group: Barnabas and John should go to Cyprus and Paul was to join forces with Silas, a leader of the Jerusalem church and well qualified for the demanding work ahead.

The Vision at Troas, 16:6–10

Paul and Silas were later joined by a staunch ally, Timothy. Follow on the map (p. 6) the journey of the three companions from Lystra to Troas. It is a strange zigzag. Luke tells us frustratingly little about it. The reference to the guidance of the Spirit may best help to explain the odd shifts of direction. Paul obviously wanted to go to the great cities of the eastern part of the province of Asia. But he felt impelled to move on, forbidden (as he puts it) by the Spirit to remain in the province. Paul may be called "The Man the Spirit Mastered." He felt he had no real freedom until his will was caught up into the will of God.

Many people today speak about being led directly by the Spirit. It is easier for most of us, perhaps, to speak rather of a hunch, a hankering, a feeling, or a yearning. These may be our equivalents of Paul's language. So we should take seriously the hunch or hankering of a sensitive person.

Finally Paul's party came to Troas. Troas was a busy port city not far from the site of ancient Troy. Its streets were thronged with merchants and sailors from east and west. To the east of the city lay the hinterland of Asia, to the west the Aegean Sea—and Greece and Europe. What direction should the apostle take? He had a dream and saw a man in Macedonian dress calling for help. A sensitive man like Paul interpreted the dream as nothing less than a disclosure of the Spirit.

Events at Philippi, 16:11–40

In a quite unassuming way Luke introduces himself into the story, for in 16:10 the so-called "we" passages begin. Thus by the time Paul left Troas, another companion had joined the travelers: Luke, the author of the book itself and of the Gospel that bears his name. Many sections of Acts from this point on sound like extracts from Luke's personal diary.

1) *The first European convert.* The travelers reached Philippi, a city with which Luke had close connections. The city lacked a synagogue, but the Jews assembled for their worship in an enclosed place at the river. Here Paul made his first convert on European soil, a woman in the purple dye trade. Her house later became the home of the four missionaries.

2) *A victim of exploitation.* Many good things were done in the city. Luke is silent about these, however, and passes at once to the

events which led to the expulsion of the missionaries. A young girl
described as a medium or fortune-teller was making good money
for her masters, possibly a body of pagan priests. She was clearly a
victim of exploitation. Paul, angered either at her incessant yelling
or at her exploiters, invoked the name of Jesus Christ and released
her from the captivity of body and mind which had crippled her as
a free, thinking human being. With this change she lost either the
will or the ability to prophesy the future. Her employers sought
revenge on Paul, and in a traversty of justice he and Silas were
stripped, flogged, and imprisoned on a charge of disturbing the peace
by advocating an unlawful religion.

3) *Release from jail.* The story of the release of Paul and his
companions from jail is one of the best known in Acts. Earthquakes
are not unknown in this area. The shock of one during the night
rocked the whole prison, flung open the doors of the cells, and
loosened the chains of the prisoners. The jailer, unnerved by the
tremor and terrified that he had lost his charges, was on the point
of killing himself. A hasty explanation of their own faith by the
apostles and a summons to trust their Lord brought the jailer to a
crucial decision which an undisturbed evening would never have
provided.

On the following day the accusations against the missionaries
were dropped, probably in the hope that they would slip quietly
out of town. Paul, however, pressed his rights as a Roman citizen.
It was said in those days that to fetter a Roman citizen was a crime
and to scourge him a scandal. Then Paul and Silas left the city,
taking Timothy but leaving Luke to work in the young church.

INSIGHTS FROM THE EVENTS AT PHILIPPI

1) *Faith and economics.* Many of our burning problems today
are really very old. The account of events at Philippi introduces us
to a constantly recurring question: How does the Christian faith
affect the realm of economics?

The conversion of the young fortune-teller had robbed her exploiters of their profits. The good news of Jesus can be social dyna-

mite when it raises questions about the ways in which money is earned or spent. It can be a serious threat to our own personal economic security or to that of our nation.

The nations of the west can spend over $100 billion for armaments each year and still grow wealthier by from four to five percent. Yet for half the inhabitants of the world the annual income is less than $700. If we really gave body to our faith in Jesus to adjust the disproportions of the world, we could expect trouble! And if this adjustment meant robbing the modern exploiters of their profit, there would certainly be protests at such a moral revolution. Would any dare to suggest such a thing? (If you are interested in exploring this subject in some detail, the study book *Rich Man Poor Man* by Donald W. Shriver, Jr. [John Knox Press, 1972] raises and suggests some answers to basic questions in this area.)

2) *The song at midnight.* Paul and Silas had been stripped, beaten, and chained, but in the middle of the night they prayed and sang hymns to God (16:25). No complaints, no groaning in self-pity—that is the authentic note of the early church. The praise we offer in dark and bleak times is a witness to faith in the risen Christ. "It is better to light a candle than to curse the darkness"—in a profound sense that is what worship means in the Christian community.

3) *The offer made in the gospel.* Paul's response to the jailer's frightened question discloses the offer which is made in the gospel of Christ. The jailer was terrified by the earthquake and fearful of being punished for his failure to guard his prisoners. In panic he asked, in effect, "Who can save me?" (16:30) Paul's answer was at a deeper level than the jailer probably had in mind with his question.

People today don't ask the jailer's question, but they are often as fearful as he of nameless destructive powers: Will I be overwhelmed, will I be destroyed—by personal failure, by unemployment, by nuclear war? Jesus is still to be proclaimed as the Savior of the world, the Savior of men and women in their failures, losses, and fears, the Savior who bridges the gap between what we are and what we can become.

4) *Preaching, faith, and baptism.* As so often in Acts, in this passage a close connection exists between preaching, faith, and baptism. Faith, as Paul says, comes by hearing, and to be baptized with water and the Spirit is to be brought into the believing community. It is possible that Paul and Silas celebrated with the jailer and his family their first communion (16:34).

PAUL AT ATHENS, 17:16–34

When Paul entered Athens, two worlds met. Of all the cities of ancient Greece none was more famous than Athens. Five centuries before Paul it had successfully led at Marathon the united counter-attack on the invading and far stronger Persian army and thus protected its independence and prepared the soil for the flowering of its democracy, art, science, philosophy, and poetry.

Athens is the mother of the arts of civilization. Here had lived the soldier-statesman Pericles, the philosopher Plato, the dramatists Aeschylus, Sophocles, and Euripides, the sculptors Phidias and Praxiteles. Here stood the Acropolis to the south of the city, dominated by the Parthenon. Ralph Waldo Emerson wrote: "Earth proudly wears the Parthenon as the best gem upon her zone." To stand at this sacred spot is to see one of the most beautiful sights in the world. But Athens in Paul's day was part of a conquered land, living much in the past.

Paul, I suspect, saw little of the beauty of Athens. Trained to worship God in worship bare of images, he could not help regarding the majestic works of art around him as idols (17:16).

Wherever there was opportunity Paul presented his message—Jesus and the resurrection. In the synagogue and the agora (the open place in the city center) he disputed like a second Socrates with Jew and Gentile.

Some of his sophisticated hearers in the agora thought he was introducing new gods, Jesus and Anastasis (the Greek word for resurrection). Such outlandish teaching inevitably brought him to the attention of the authorities, and he was taken to the council of the Areopagus, which had powers to deal with moral questions and matters of public order (17:19).

The speech of Paul before the council is a brilliant summary of his message to the Greeks. It is not, of course, the complete message word-for-word, but it expresses Paul's authentic voice.

1) *A point of contact established.* The speech impresses us at once with the way the apostle established contact with his hearers. In verses 22–29 we listen to Paul adapting himself to the situation of his audience. He compliments them on their deep interest in religious questions. He comments on the inscription he had observed on a sacred monument, the very wording of which was a sign of unfulfilled religious yearning. He quotes from authorities already familiar to his hearers, the Stoic philosopher Cleanthes and the poet Aratus.

The true proclamation of Christ does not destroy all that already exists in the life or culture of those to whom it comes. In words which were widely used in the Middle Ages, grace perfects, it does not destroy nature. We can never "bring God" to the world. What we can do is try to show how the ever present God has constantly disclosed himself within each part of man's life and culture.

2) *The apostle's summons.* We see next how the apostle thrusts his message home. Without fear or favor Paul accuses his Athenian hearers (them of all people!) of *ignorance*. They did not know (How could they, since the fullness of truth is known only in Christ?) that the living God calls on all people to respond to him. Through the ages God has passed over men's ignorance, but now he summons them to respond to his encounter with the world in Christ. (Read 17:30–31.) We respond to God through repentance and faith, a repentance that turns us from all that makes us less than ourselves to the Lord of the world, who creates all things new, and a faith that reaches out to hold the risen Jesus.

3) *Different responses to the gospel.* Some at the council burst out laughing. The rest were apparently in favor of adjourning the meeting without an immediate decision. But some accepted the truth in what Paul was saying (17:32–34).

There are always some for whom the gospel is ridiculous or sheer wishful thinking. Others postpone a firm decision on it. But there has also always been the miracle of faith leaping to life. There are the unknown in every group who cling to the truth which they hear in the gospel and whose lives are affected by its offer of life to the full in Christ (see John 10:10).

4) *The cost of discipleship.* Though we do not learn from Acts how much his ministry in Athens took out of him, Paul speaks elsewhere of the cost of this kind of discipleship. The Athens experience sapped the strength even of Paul. Writing later to the Corinthians he says, "I was with you in weakness and in much fear and trembling." (1 Cor. 2:3) Athens had done that to him.

5) *The beginnings of a profound relationship.* At Athens the world of Paul hit against the world of Greece. At Athens a relationship began that was to endure to the present time in one form or another—the relation between faith and secular learning, between the resurrection and human reason, between the gospel and contemporary culture. Any attempt today to explain the meaning of the gospel in terms of modern ways of thought or life is part of a process that had its beginnings in Athens.

The Athens experience marked the start of the attempt to build bridges between faith and reason, to explain the faith in reasoned statements, to show how the Christian gospel is the true wisdom after which the best of minds have been groping.

FOR THOUGHT AND DISCUSSION

At the beginning of the chapter the issue of faith and economics was raised. The first two passages which follow represent different ideas of what exploitation means.

In 1960, 620,000 Californians were receiving some form of welfare payments. Today, 2.4 million are on the welfare rolls, costing California taxpayers $3 billion a year.

The number on relief has quadrupled in ten years. One out of nine now receives welfare. By 1972 it is expected to be one out of seven.

In California more than 70 percent of the welfare load is caused, in part or in full, by absent fathers. These men should be hunted down and compelled to support their offspring. There is no reason for the taxpayers to continue to support illegitimate children. The truth is that illegitimacy is not only supported, but encouraged by welfare practices.

Howard E. Kershner, "Look Ahead America" [1]

I believe that we could reasonably call the relationship between the United States and the developing world exploitative if two conditions were met. First, we would need to show that the nature of the world's present—and arbitrary—economic order, including the institutions which sustain it, is such as to work toward a permanent widening of the division between rich and poor nations, as well as toward generally chaotic economic conditions in developing states. Second, we would have to demonstrate that the United States is in a systematic way working to preserve this economic order. . . . The evidence is persuasive that the United States is working to preserve an international economic order which systematically works to the disadvantage of developing nations; and by my earlier definition, this constitutes a form of "exploitation" of these nations.

David S. French, "Does the U.S. Exploit the Developing Nations?" [2]

The issues raised in these allegations are complex. Some members of the class will have to do research on the question. What are the forms of exploitation known to you? What are the special moral issues in the American economic system? What points of influence does the individual Christian have access to for affecting the economic system? Does Paul's encounter with the fortune-teller give you any insights?

The writer of the third passage asks us to consider the meaning of "Paul in Chains." The writer himself was imprisoned because, as he argues, he had become a source of discomfort to the forces of law and order. He asks us, who is the truly free man, and who is in bondage?

Are not the prisoner and the astronaut two interesting American symbols today? The question, as put, is very nearly unanswerable, and to that extent meaningless. What is really of point is the contention that American outer-space exploration, with the book of Genesis resounding throughout the universe, is an activity that approaches the blasphemous. It is relieved of malice only by the unrelieved and very nearly incurable innocence of those who take part in such paraliturgy [a kind of secular act of worship]. For the fact is that outer space itself, and the innovative scientific activity of the great powers there, is almost totally claimed by the military. In comparison with all this, the immobility of the man in jail, whose mind is supple before experience, is highly preferable. For at least it can be said of such a man that he is offered a measure of space and of purity within which to imagine a form of life worthy of the human.

Daniel Berrigan, *No Bars to Manhood* [3]

Does this extract help you to a better understanding of Paul's response to his imprisonment at Philippi? How does one keep his mind "supple before experience"? Are you free, or imprisoned, or a bit of both?

The final passage is a moving testimony of faith by Kenneth Clark.

At this point I reveal myself in my true colours, as a stick-in-the-mud. I hold a number of beliefs that have been repudiated by the liveliest intellects of our time. I believe that order is better than chaos, creation better than destruction. I prefer gentleness to violence, forgiveness to vendetta. On the whole I think that knowledge is preferable to ignorance, and I am sure that human sympathy is more valuable than ideology. I believe that in spite of the recent triumphs of science, men haven't changed much in the last two thousand years; and in consequence we must still try to learn from history. History is ourselves. I also hold one or two beliefs that are more difficult to put shortly. For example, I believe in courtesy, the ritual by which we avoid hurting other people's feelings by satisfying our own egos. And I think we

should remember that we are part of a great whole, which for
convenience we call nature. All living things are our brothers
and sisters. Above all, I believe in the God-given genius of certain individuals, and I value a society that makes their existence
possible.

Kenneth Clark, *Civilisation*[4]

The "civilization" of which the writer speaks is a rich and in-
finitely varied blend of Christian values and classical culture. How
important should it be to us to study the ancient world for a richer
knowledge of truth and beauty? What should our attitude be to the
quest for wisdom (wherever it may be found) or the creation of
lovely things? Is it important to our society to honor these pursuits?
Does ugliness offend you? Why, and why do you think something is
ugly? What light does Paul's ministry in Athens throw on these
questions?

8

Always Roaming with a Hungry Heart
Acts 18:1—20:12

T HE PACE OF the missionary journey quickens. The restlessness of Paul is astonishing, almost beyond belief. He was like the Ulysses of Tennyson's vision: "I cannot rest from travel . . . always roaming with a hungry heart." Paul's hunger was to win people over by his gospel, until Christ should be formed in them.

PAUL ARRIVES AT CORINTH, 18:1–11

Paul left Athens and came to Corinth. It was like passing from one world to another. Athens was the metropolis of the arts and wisdom; Corinth, the largest and wealthiest city in Greece, was a bustling center of trade, commerce, and pleasure. In the temple of the goddess of love a thousand sacred prostitutes served her worshipers. A Latin proverb, "Not everyone has the good luck to go to Corinth," referred to the notorious vices of the city. But even in Corinth the life and healing of Christ were to be offered.

Paul lodged at the home of a Jewish couple named Aquila and Priscilla, resident aliens who had lately come to the city as refugees from Rome. The two, like Paul, were tentmakers by trade. He was joined also by Silas and Timothy, and their arrival in the spring must have been a consolation for his rejection in the synagogue. The three collaborated in writing, to the Thessalonian church, Letters which throw bright light on the gains and sufferings of a hectic year. To many of his friends in Corinth Paul later paid a lovely tribute; see Romans 16:3, 23.

A Journey Ends and Begins
at Ephesus, 18:18–21, 19:8–10

Paul was dominated by the urge to move on, to expand the scope of his apostolic mission. From Corinth he traveled with Priscilla and Aquila to Ephesus, and from there to Caesarea and then to Antioch. Almost without pause, it seems he set out once more, and a new journey began, usually called the "third." The city of Ephesus became his base of operations.

The gospel had been introduced into Ephesus before Paul came. In 18:19–21 we read of the strengthening of the earlier foundation. Paul was constantly active. It was from Ephesus that he wrote his first Letter to the Corinthian church. Unfortunately, Paul's preaching led to an unhappy breach with the synagogue. The passage on the division tells us much about the nature of the church.

1) *The church is a witness to and bearer of the kingdom of God* (see 19:8). The church is always a pilgrim church, a people "of the Way," a society in fellowship with God that prepares for the coming of his kingdom. In its own common life it already anticipates and experiences that kingdom. So the heart of its proclamation is that rule of God which is the inward and outward transformation of the whole earth, indeed, of the whole creation itself.

2) *The church is a teaching church.* Paul's theme at Ephesus was old but ever new—repentance and faith in Jesus Christ (20:20–21). The church's task is to unfold what in practice this means in each age. Through Christ a new life has become available in which men and women can gain true freedom—the freedom to do what is good and to serve God. Repentance and faith are the roads by which we have access to this life "in the Spirit."

3) *Faithful proclamation of this new way will inevitably draw down upon itself resentment and opposition* (see 19:9). The gospel comes to us with its offer (the freedom of the "life and more than life" that Christ brings) and its demand (repentance). But the demand will always be resented by some because of the changes of life and thinking it calls for.

A Crisis at Ephesus, 19:21–41

The commentary on Paul's Letter to the Romans which was published in 1918 by the Swiss theologian Karl Barth was described by one observer as "a bomb flung in the playground of the theologians." The uproar described in Acts 19 could be called the result of the bomb flung in the bazaar of the silversmiths. The bomb, of course, was Paul's courageous preaching, which pulled down false gods and defied false loyalties.

It has been suggested that the passage from 19:21 to the end of Acts may be called the passion or sufferings of Paul. It does not describe his death but the steps which led up to it. The parallels to the end of the Gospels are striking.

The cause of the trouble is clear. In Ephesus there was a silversmith's guild which manufactured, at no little profit, silver shrines of the local goddess Artemis. But Paul's strict monotheism—the denial that any save God is to be worshiped—had been bad for local business. Complaints had been voiced by one leader, Demetrius.

Two of Paul's companions were hauled into the vast open-air theater by some hooligans (no doubt paid well for their work). The two escaped only by the skin of their teeth. A Jew named Alexander who tried to put in a word was hooted down. Paul himself was only dissuaded from interfering by the Asiarchs, the city officials responsible for emperor worship. At a later time Paul recalled that he had fought with beasts at Ephesus (1 Cor. 15:32), which may be a vivid way of referring to the riot.

Are there not forces at work today comparable to those Paul confronted?

1) *Idolatry.* Modern communities can hardly be said to be troubled by the idolatry that existed in Ephesus. Yet when we translate their situation into our own terms, we sometimes hear sounds we do not like. If we give supreme loyalty to something other than God—whether it be to a personal aim, an idea, or a cause—we have put the worship of the creature into the place of the Creator. An idol, as Joy Davidman has reminded us, is not just an image. It is something which we manipulate in order to get what we want.[1]

2) *Isolationism.* The Ephesus incidents remind us also of the narrow and often fierce local politics that resents outside interference. This is the attitude that says: our way of life is precious to us, and we will not tolerate interference from outside. We want to be left alone. The outsider with his strange ideas disturbs us. In a world where the direction of history is plainly heading for a free world, united in its diversity, to resent any who preach an uncomfortable message of freedom and unity is to oppose history and thus to refuse to accept what God seems to be doing in history.

3) *Distortion of truth.* There is another contemporary problem foreshadowed in the Ephesian riot: the power to mislead by distorting truth. Any who have had experience speaking to crowds know how easy it is to anger or to stir people. In a day of instant communication the danger is multiplied. Demetrius obviously knew something about crowd psychology. He knew how to twist words slightly to protect his own pocket or security.

The church, which knows that the will of God is truth, has a kind of sentinel's duty in our world. It will try to point to the truth and warn about distortions of the truth. The real falsehoods of our time are lies of expediency, evasions of truth, and manipulations of facts—witness a great many pressure groups and lobbies that protect narrow interests; witness many political speeches; witness (sad to say) many pious statements even in the church itself.

4) *Economic self-interest.* The Ephesian episode lays bare another problem for us: the covering of economic self-interest under the cloak of idealism or religion. One of the most blatant illustrations of this in history was the notorious case of John Tetzel in the sixteenth century. He sold indulgences for his employer by which, he boasted, complete remission of sins was obtained even for those in purgatory. The Tetzel scandal finally produced the revolt of Martin Luther. In one of his sermons Tetzel played on the tender feelings and fears of his audience: "Don't you hear the voices of your wailing dead parents and others [in purgatory] who say, 'Have mercy upon me'?" [2] Little wonder he made a mint for his master out of the gullible! What are our equivalents?

To be aware of these problems—of which we have named only a few—is at least half the battle. The clue to resolving them is in the statement attributed to Paul in 19:26. Perhaps more than ever today we must think of the apostolic gospel and the Christian life as a "counter-culture" which refuses to accept many aspects of our politics, our public morality, or our economics as right or normal.

FAREWELL TO GREECE, 20:1–6

There is a sad line by a poet: "Look thy last on all things lovely." [3] Something of this emotion wells up in these few verses, which read like extracts from a traveler's diary. Paul had made up his mind to go to Rome, but he still had much to do. So he said good-bye to the disciples at Ephesus and set out for Macedonia. We know from his Second Letter to the Corinthians that Titus joined him at Philippi (2 Cor. 7:5–7).

The summer and fall were spent visiting communities of believers across the mainland of Greece, giving them encouragement and helping also to raise funds for the Jerusalem church. Three months of winter were spent mostly in Corinth. When winter storms ended and the navigation lanes were open again, Paul and his party embarked for Syria, perhaps with pilgrims bound for the Passover festival in Jerusalem. But a plot against Paul (murder at sea?) was uncovered, and he went by land to Philippi, where Luke rejoined the party. They were all to rendezvous later in Troas.

THE SUNDAY SERVICE AT TROAS, 20:7–12

With the memory of the recent Passover celebrations still with them Paul now celebrated the eucharist or Lord's Supper with the community of believers at Troas. The passage is well known for the incident of the fall of Eutychus from a third-story window and the report of his miraculous recovery. Of much more interest to us today is the glimpse given of a (presumably) typical Sunday service of the early church. Some elements in the account should be noted.

1) *The day of resurrection.* The worship is described as taking place on the first day of the week (20:7). This was the day cele-

brating the resurrection of Jesus Christ. The first day of the week, according to ancient reckoning, began at sunset, a time suitable for those who had been working during the day to attend the Christian liturgy. Many of these worshipers, like Eutychus, would probably be tired. Since the service began on what we should call Saturday evening, lights were needed, and still today the use of lights and candles at worship reminds us of our bond with the early church.

2) *The day of fellowship.* The day is described as one of meeting, or assembling, or gathering together (20:7). It is the day of fellowship in love and truth, a fellowship realized through the Spirit who gathers the people of God into a unity.

3) *The day of eucharist.* The day is also described as one of breaking bread or eucharist (20:7). It is likely (as we know from evidence outside the New Testament) that a meal or banquet was served in the evening, followed either then or at dawn the next morning by the eucharist itself.

The worship of this day included the ministry of the Word—in Paul's case his preaching was prolonged until midnight. Where friends meet knowing it may be for the last time, there is always something more to say. Samuel Rutherford once said, "I had but one eye, one joy, one delight, ever to preach Christ." Paul would have recognized a brother in Rutherford.

FOR THOUGHT AND DISCUSSION

The first issue to be discussed is the relation between the church and the kingdom of God—the theme of the first selection.

While there is an inseparable relationship between the Kingdom and the church, they are not to be identified. The Kingdom takes its point of departure from God, the church from men. The Kingdom is God's reign and the realm in which the blessings of his reign are experienced; the church is the fellowship of those who have experienced God's reign and entered into the enjoyment of its blessings. The Kingdom creates the church, works through the church, and is proclaimed in the world by the church. There can be no Kingdom without a church—those who have acknowledged God's rule—and there can be no church without God's Kingdom. . . .

George Elton Ladd, *Jesus and the Kingdom* [4]

Discuss what you think the writer means. Is it the church's mission to witness to the kingdom of God? Do we need to belong to the church to belong to the kingdom? Are there "anonymous Christians" who don't belong to any church? How do you relate your citizenship in the kingdom of God to your loyalty to your nation?

The second extract tries to bring up-to-date the practical problems of the Ephesian silversmiths.

The [Vietnam] war began to be a significant and conscious source of gain to particular economic interests in this country. At first that meant the corporations supplying the goods and services of the war itself—construction firms, and firms producing the weapons and equipment and supplies of the American and Vietnamese military. But, as with the spread of the Roman Empire (among others), activity at the frontiers soon came to require and suggest associated commercial, industrial and financial activities. Somewhat later, the area began to promise good returns for investment. (Last month, *The Wall Street Journal* announced that four additional corporations were planning to set up plants in South Vietnam; among these are Coca-Cola and Ford.) . . . In short, all sectors and functions of the American economy—business, agriculture, industry, commerce, finance, labor, and our economic rhythms—now connect somewhat or greatly to our little economy in South Vietnam.

Douglas F. Dowd, "The Political Economy of War" [5]

Do you generally agree or disagree with the writer's views? Either way, how would *you* translate the account of the Ephesian silversmiths into modern terms? What parallels to the idols of Ephesus would you find in our own society? Are we in danger of saying, "Great is Coca-Cola," or "Great is Ford"?

The third extract comes from a book on the future of the

Christian Sunday. The writer argues that there should be four characteristics of Sunday activities: freedom, joy, recreation, and cre-
ativity.

If Sunday activities have these four qualities, they will be
play. Play stands over against work in the freedom with which
it is done, in the more intense joy it provides, in the recreation
of mind and body which it affords, and in its creativeness which
produces something personal, whether this be as transient as a
well-made serve in a tennis-match or as permanent as an oil
painting. And if Sunday activities are play, then they are appropriate for the celebration of the paschal mystery* and the
new creation. The question which the Christian should ask about
his Sunday activity comes down to this: Is this activity play
for me? If it is, then it is suitable for the day without further
question. If it is doubtful, then he should go ahead with it in the
spirit of play with the intention of celebrating the new creation;
he should make it play.

The pastoral strategy suggested here for preserving the Sunday observance of rest does not consist in decrying those who
work on Sunday, in repeating the ancient injunctions against
work, in pointing out the evils which will befall men if they work
on Sunday, in boycotting shopping centers open on Sunday, or
in pressuring legislatures to pass laws against work on Sunday.
Some of these tactics, at times, may be appropriate in particular
situations. But in the long run it is more important to disseminate
a very positive understanding of Sunday rest as celebration of
the paschal mystery by play in the new creation.

Christopher Kiesling, *The Future of the Christian Sunday*[6]

Do you agree that the writer has a "positive understanding of
Sunday rest"? Contrast the pattern he commends with your activities on several recent Sundays. Compare both with the description
of the Sunday service at Ephesus.

---

* By "paschal mystery," the writer means the celebration of Christ's resurrection, especially in the Lord's Supper or Eucharist.

9

Passage to Jerusalem
Acts 20:17—23:11

T HE COMPANIONS WERE pressing to be in Jerusalem for Pentecost within thirty days—not too long a time, for ancient cargo
vessels averaged only three or four knots, and that only on good sailing days. At Miletus Paul bade farewell for the last time to the elders
or presbyters of Ephesus.

THE CHARGE TO THE EPHESIAN ELDERS, 20:17–38

The speech is without equal in Acts. It shows us Paul at the
peak of his powers as a leader, pastor, and preacher. It has a passion
and an authority, a tact and yet an anxiety in the face of human
weaknesses, that only a Paul could have expressed. Intensely personal, typically Pauline, it has every mark of true, apostolic boldness.
We may analyze the speech in the following way.

1) *Review and defense of his ministry.* Paul had nothing to be
ashamed of in accounting for his service of the gospel. Such ministry
is always a costly thing: it drains the energies of body and mind.
Tears and difficulties had been no strangers to Paul (20:19). The
true minister is not "on call" only at certain times, but is a man or
a woman totally committed to the service of the people of God day
and night (20:31).

John Knox, the leader of the Scottish Reformation, was captured
by the French and chained to the oars of a galley for nineteen
months. "How long," he once wrote in a rare unveiling of that night-
mare, "how long I continued prisoner, what torment I sustained in

the galleys, and what were the sobs of my heart, is now no time to recite." [1] Paul would have recognized that brand of suffering.

And for what? Why was this man willing to pay any cost without flinching? It was because he was the servant of Christ, and his service was that of teaching and bearing witness to the gospel of grace, calling men to repentance and faith, and declaring the whole counsel of God (20:20-21, 24).

2) *Review of his prospects.* There was little real security for such a man. He had no idea what would happen to him (20:22, 24). Even life was not precious to him—not a thing to waste words on—if only he could fulfill his mission. Risk and sorrow are at the heart of apostolic service.

3) *Commission to the church's leaders.* Paul had an urgent piece of advice for the leaders of the Ephesian church, and it was twice repeated: be on guard (20:28, 31). Did Paul not trust those who came to him from Ephesus? Was he being bitter, or simply realistic? He knew that there would be distortions of the truth, failures, and betrayals in the life of the church. Unfair allegations would be made. He himself had had personal experience of that (20:33-34). A wry but apt comment was once made by someone who loved the church but knew its shortcomings: "It takes a great deal of courage to support a cause when you see some of the others who support it with you."

4) *Paul's farewell.* The speech had the character of a last will and testament. Paul would see them no more. Could there be a better expression of love than his final benediction (20:32)? God would build in Ephesus something more beautiful than the temple of Artemis, he would enrich them with something more valuable than the wealth of the temple treasury.

THE ARRIVAL AT JERUSALEM, 21:15-40

On his arrival at Jerusalem, Paul was given a warm welcome by James and the brothers. But hostility was seething in the city, and his opponents were ready to pounce. The shell that covers brutality in a civilized society is dangerously fragile. A scene of mob violence like that described in this passage reminds us how easily human communities can be put into confusion.

A gang from Ephesus, who had been nursing their wrath for such a time as this, rushed upon Paul when he came into the temple to perform an act of devotion. Either they or those who had hired them for their job were convinced that Paul had utterly betrayed the religious tradition of the Jews. If it was a savage and mindless act, so are all attempts at assassination.

Soon the whole city was in a turmoil, and it was only with considerable difficulty that the Roman commanding officer intervened to rescue Paul from being lynched. A brief inquiry was held, and Paul was taken for protection toward the fortress of Antonia. In a bold move that might well have proved fatal Paul asked permission to address the crowd.

Paul's Defense and
the Renewal of the Frenzy, 22:1–29

Shortly after the Russian Revolution at a mass meeting in Moscow, speaker after speaker praised the massive changes in society that had been brought about. Bitter hostility was vented against the old regime. A thin, undernourished priest, whose very dress made him suspect, asked leave to speak. He began, "You have heard all the arguments which have been brought forward to prove the new world view. But my dear brothers, *Christos woskrese!* (Christ is risen)." [2] It is a story in which many of the elements found in this passage of Acts are repeated: a hostile crowd, a daring speech, the gospel of the resurrection.

1) *Paul's starting point.* Paul could have had only one starting point: the Damascus road. Twenty years had passed, but its vividness was undimmed. Indeed, the account which we read here (actually the second of three versions in Acts) is more complete than the others. Also, the memory of the man to whose lynching he had consented—Stephen—was burned on his mind.

Paul's Gospel was from the first a thoroughly personal gospel. It arose out of his own history. At the end of his score for the oratorio, *The Dream of Gerontius,* Edward Elgar wrote, "This I saw and knew." Paul could have said that about the resurrection. But his resurrection gospel was not something for himself alone; it had to be shared, for the Easter message has a universal character. The words of Ananias to Paul, which he quoted in his speech, could be taken as a motto for the whole people of God: "you will be a witness for him to all men of what you have seen and heard." (22:15)

2) *The hated name.* The crowd remained silent until Paul described his vision in the temple, but the atmosphere was heavy with danger. Within the speech was the spark which produced the explosion. It was the hated word "Gentile" that made the crowd howl for his blood.

Simple words like this can ignite fiery reaction. Mob leaders know how to sway popular opinion because they understand that an angry crowd thinks with its blood. Prejudice is an unreasoning act, and the right abusive term spoken at the desired moment can be calculated to stimulate the sought for hate. Nigger, Dago, honkie, Uncle Tom, red neck, hippie, Communist, pig, Polack—words like these can be sparks in an explosive air. The use of such emotional words bypasses caution and fair judgments.

Quite unconsciously, perhaps, Paul had used a word which stimulated that kind of response in his hearers. The word "Gentile" had been festering in the mind of the crowd because it summed up a total attitude to people unlike themselves: Gentiles were heretics, rebels, things to flout. Only a massive transformation of values can change the outlook of those who think about other people in slogans and threats.

BEFORE THE SUPREME COUNCIL, 22:30—23:10

From prison Paul was brought before the supreme council in Jerusalem. He had no sooner started to speak to his inquisitors, a little tactlessly perhaps, than the high priest, Ananias, ordered him to be struck on the mouth. A blistering retort from Paul quickly gave way to a cooler mood and a saner judgment.

The topic of debate Paul deliberately chose was one likely to divide the participants angrily: the resurrection of the dead. The Sadducees denied the belief, while the Pharisees affirmed it. Since Paul's own message from the first had been "Jesus and the resurrection," there was some sympathy for him from the Pharisees, though little real understanding of his outlook.

Two insights can be gained from Paul's appearance before the council.

1) *The meaning of grace.* The account teaches us a valuable lesson on God's grace. Paul's anger surprises us initially. Even though we realize that the charged atmosphere was bound to have unnerved him, he emerges in the account as a very human figure. We like our heroes to be without blemish, and we tend to be critical of lapses in those from whom we expect better things. It is fatally easy to be critical of someone's outward failures and even to find a furtive joy in his or her downfall.

Paul was a giant, with the courage of a lion and a restless zeal for his gospel. He was tender and strong. He was haunted by a driving passion—the service of Jesus. But in this passage he displayed only too "human" characteritics: boastfulness, or at least tactlessness (23:1), anger (23:3), perhaps even falsehood (23:5)— it's hard to believe that Paul did not know the customs of the council or did not recognize the high priest.

Our trouble is that we do not think a good man or woman should ever fall like this. But they do, and it should not surprise us. To begin to live "in grace" doesn't mean that we immediately are better than we were or believe more. It means to discover that we are acceptable to God *as we are.* However much we may be debtors, God declares that we are creditable. By sheer grace!

2) *The sin of religious men.* We find another insight in the passage: it is about the anger of religious men, or, more briefly, about sin.

F. W. Faber, the nineteenth-century English theologian and

hymn writer, once said: "Religious people, as a whole, are an unkind lot." How was it possible that men steeped in the faith of the Scriptures could become party to what was almost a lynching (23:9–10)? Some of them even consented to a cold-blooded assassination plot (23:12–15). They thought of Paul, of course, as a monstrous betrayer of their tradition. But in opposing him they had themselves become monsters.

A missionary in India who lived in the squalor and disease of his people accused the nations of the west for failing to help to lift up that low society from its poverty. He spoke of the "immorality" of the west—of its squandering of astronomical sums on war and space and giving only a pittance to alleviate poverty. The extremity of the accusation was offensive to many in the churches which supported him. Yet is there not always the possibility that those who think themselves "righteous" by any normal stands may indeed be party to a vast crime against humanity? Is our failure to feed the hungry millions of mankind an example? Is failure to speak out on the issue of the sacredness of all life another? Are there not circumstances in which we can become party to a sin so vast that we fail to see the connection between it and our faith?

A Consoling Vision, 23:11

A vision like this is not something seen so much as something experienced. We sometimes say, when an insight becomes plain, "It came to me. . . ." A writer like Luke would not use such abstract language. He prefers to make it personal and say that the Lord came to Paul and consoled him.

Are visions like this for us? St. John of the Cross says that in ordinary human experience there are times when a curtain falls away and a wisdom comes to us which we cannot understand. In a precarious situation it may come to us that we really are safe, whatever may happen outwardly. In a time of loneliness or hurt it may come to us that we really are loved; it dawns on me that this person loves *me*. What a surprise! Such a love is grace—not just amazing, but surprising and free and transforming. So grace is

experienced as comfort, hope, and affection. It keeps us, as it kept
Paul, going on.

FOR THOUGHT AND DISCUSSION

The first passage to be discussed speaks (as Paul had spoken to
the Ephesians) of the continual struggle to remain completely at the
service of Christ and others. It is from a prayer entitled, "The Priest:
A Prayer on Sunday Night," but it can express also the feelings of
all who share the priestly ministry of Christ.

Lord, I'm thirty-five years old,
A body made like others,
Arms ready for work,
A heart meant for love,
But I've given you all ...
It's hard to be nothing to oneself in order to be everything to
    others.
It's hard to be like others, among others, and to be other.
It's hard always to give without trying to receive.
It's hard to seek out others and to be, oneself, unsought.
It's hard to suffer from the sins of others, and yet be obliged to
    hear and bear them.
It's hard to be told secrets, and be unable to share them.
It's hard to carry others and never, even for a moment, be
    carried.
It's hard to sustain the feeble and never be able to lean on one
    who is strong.
It's hard to be alone,
Alone before everyone,
Alone before the world,
Alone before suffering,
    death,
    sin.

*   *   *

Son, you are not alone,
I am with you;

I am you.
For I needed another human instrument to continue my Incar-
    nation and my Redemption.
Out of all eternity, I chose you,
I need you.
I need your hands to continue to bless,
I need your lips to continue to speak,
I need your body to continue to suffer,
I need your heart to continue to love,
I need you to continue to save,
Stay with me, son.

Michel Quoist, Prayers [3]

Does this help you to understand Paul's own ministry? What does it say to you about your own ministry? Through what human channels does Christ support you? Whom do you support in his name? What other means of mutual spiritual support would be desirable?

In the second passage the writer helps us to understand the "anatomy of violence." He is quoting from an account of the Watts riot of 1965.

> In the manner with which the police had handled the girl the people saw, or thought they saw, the contempt of the white man for the Negro. They felt, collectively, his heel grinding in their faces. They were stricken once more by the sting of his power. . . .

> The Riot Commission's "cumulative chain" had reached its last link. An incident had been generated which symbolized for those present every ounce of humiliation, every nuance of hope-lessness, every hurt to pride, self-esteem, and loyalty possible. . . .

> Without conscious thought of his action [one man] darted into the street and hurled the empty pop bottle in his hand toward the last of the departing black-and-white cars. Strik-ing the rear fender of Sgt. Rankin's car, it shattered. And it was as if in that shattering the thousand people lining the

street found their own release. It was as if in one violent contortion the bonds of restraint were snapped. Rocks, bottles, pieces of wood and iron—whatever missiles came to hand—were projected against the sides and windows of the bus and automobiles that, halted for the past 20 minutes by the jammed street, unwittingly started through the gauntlet. . . .

Once collective action has been initiated, it acquires a momentum of its own; even if people did not suffer from grievances, riots would attract and recruit participants. They would do so because they appeal to boredom, anger, frustration, desire for adventure; because they provide a ready-made opportunity to discharge feelings.

Hans Toch, *Violent Men* [4]

Do you see any parallels between this and the account of the Jerusalem riot on account of Paul? Are there common elements in each account—for example, the angry crowd (What makes the crowd angry?), acts of brutality (or necessity?), and the word or deed that arouses the crowd to violence? If you had been in the Jerusalem crowd, how do you think you would have reacted? in the Watts crowd?

In Spite of the Gates of Hell

Acts 23:12—25:12

J UST BEFORE LUTHER entered the city of Worms, summoned to appear before the emperor and facing not only a trial of his views but possible assassination also, he wrote to his friend Melanchthon: "I shall enter Worms under Christ's leadership in spite of the gates of hell." [1] That is courage. Dangers for Paul when summoned before the supreme council in Jerusalem were no less threatening. During the trial itself he had come into collision with the Sadducees. The Sadducees were the aristocratic, reactionary party, not above using violence if necessary. At the end of the hearing forty men had bound themselves by oath to kill the apostle (23:12).

A PLOT DETECTED: PAUL IN CUSTODY, 23:12–35

The fanatical party in the supreme council had worked its will. To achieve their end they entered into collaboration with the popular party. The coalition may be called "the establishment." They were in power. They were also in fear. Paul was a public enemy and he had to be destroyed. The establishment always protects itself, by persuasion if possible, by violence if necessary (23:12–15). But the plot to assassinate Paul was revealed through his nephew, a sign that some at least of his family had been reconciled to him. More than normal precautions were necessary, and Paul was taken for custody to Caesarea, the home of the imperial provincial officer. A small army marched with him for his protection.

In Roman law the state was the avenger of offenses against

public order. Trials were conducted in the provinces by the "procurator" or delegate of the emperor. This official had broad powers to apportion the penalty according to the facts of the case. The procurator who was to hear Paul's case was Felix.

One of the most critical matters to touch our lives today is brought out in this passage—*the tension between human rights and the common good*. Read 23:12–15. It is a frightening passage. The supreme council did not consist of evil men; yet for the sake of the common good they consented to a monstrously evil act.

The episode points us back to the whole dilemma of the crucifixion itself. The parallels are disturbing because again and again in history politicians have judged that even murder may be justified to protect the state. The finding of the supreme council against Paul was the same as that of Caiaphas against Jesus: "we are ready to kill him. . . ." "It was expedient that one man should die." (Compare 23:15 with John 18:14.)

The Inquiry Before the Procurator, 24:1–23

Felix, the judge before whom Paul's inquiry was held, is known to us from other places. He was procurator of Palestine A.D. 52–59. His first wife was a granddaughter of Antony and Cleopatra. His second wife, Drusilla, was the youngest daughter of Herod Agrippa I. At the time she first met Paul she was only in her late teens.

Felix has been called "one of the worst governors Judea ever had." An ancient Roman historian says of him that he "fostered crime by misconceived remedies." This was the man who was to pass a verdict on Paul and the doctrine of the resurrection (24:21).

1) *The charge against Paul.* The spokesman for the hierarchy in the council was lawyer called Tertullus. After some flattering words of introduction he brought in the indictment. First, Paul was called a public nuisance, a promoter of world revolutions. He was politically dangerous, a conspirator against the government. Second, he was a ringleader of the Nazarenes, a sect which was threatening to overturn the old religious traditions. Third, and more specifically, he had tried to profane the temple (24:2–8).

2) *Paul's answer.* In his rebuttal Paul answered the charges one by one. He made a point of showing his respect for the orderly processes of society (24:10). He was no political revolutionary, he insisted. He had not tried to stir up a fanatical crowd (24:12). Moreover, far from depreciating the worth and honor of the Jewish tradition, "I worship the God of our fathers, believing everything laid down by the law or written in the prophets." (24:14) Lastly, he had at no time consented to the defilement of the temple (24:18). What was at issue, he argued, was the meaning of the resurrection.

The charges against Paul were not confirmed. Felix therefore adjourned the inquiry, and Paul was put into custody, though apparently with considerable freedom.

IMPLICATIONS FOR US TODAY

Again and again the indictments laid against Paul have also been laid against the followers of Jesus. Consider the following accusations which at times have been alleged against Christians.

1) *"They are political revolutionaries."* To take a present-day example, in Brazil mass problems of sickness, poverty, and illiteracy have produced serious political and ideological conflicts in the churches. Conscientious men and women who have tried to combat such critical problems as the 70 percent illiteracy rate and the 50 percent infant mortality rate have often been accused of being dangerous radicals. Yet to believe in the resurrection means to believe that God wills the whole world to come to full and healthy life.

2) *"They are overturning the old traditions."* Attempts to renew the church by changing its worship or rewriting its confessions have often been condemned as an overturning of the old traditions. Yet to believe in the resurrection means to believe that outward forms of the church must be constantly renewed in order to express the inner meaning of the gospel.

3) *"They are destroying the purity of the church."* The charge of destroying the purity of the church is easier to make than to

prove. Calvin deals with the question in a helpful way. There have always been those, he says, who have been "imbued with a false conviction of their own perfect sanctity," and who have therefore spurned to associate with those who are not perfect in every respect. (Shall we say, with those who do not subscribe to our particular confessions of faith or have our form of constitution and government?) After quoting with approval Paul's words about Christ cleansing the church (Eph. 5:25–27), Calvin goes on to comment: "Yet it is no less true that the Lord is daily at work in smoothing out wrinkles and cleansing spots. From this it follows that the church's holiness is not yet complete." [2] The only purity the church possesses is not its own but Christ's.

THE DEEPER INQUIRY OF THE PROCURATOR, 24:24–26

Paul was under inquiry by the procurator concerning his views. But in a sense it was the procurator himself who was under inquiry. For two long years—with so much therefore having to be left undone!—Paul remained a prisoner in Caesarea. Knowing how restless he was in mind and body, we can be sure he was as active as possible, teaching, writing, and arguing about "Jesus and the resurrection." From time to time during his imprisonment, Felix sent for Paul and had private discussions with him.

The theme of Paul's discussion in this passage shows us that he knew the measure of the Roman inquisitor and his consort well. Significantly, he preached on righteousness, self-control, and the coming judgment.

The greatest preaching is not always done in front of vast throngs. Sometimes it is done before one or two in a private place; it doesn't sound like a sermon, and its theme varies according to the needs of the moment and the riches of the gospel.

The passage tells us something essential about preaching: preaching is not something done in a vacuum but always in a particular human situation. Paul McCartney described in a *Life* magazine article how the troubles of the Beatles began when they stopped touring in 1966 and concentrated on recording: "So I came to the idea of going to village halls which held a couple of hundred people. . . .

Being an actual good musician requires this contact with people all the time. The human thing." [3] Preaching is like that. It requires "the human thing," "contact with people."

A POLITICAL MOVE AND AN APPEAL TO CAESAR, 24:27—25:12

The high-handed Felix was summoned to Rome to account for the misconduct of his administration. He was replaced by a man of a different caliber, Festus, an honorable man. But events were getting beyond control. Paul's still unresolved case was an unlanced boil in the body of the religious establishment.

Festus was well aware that no fair hearing could be held in Jerusalem, and Luke reports that the assassination attempt which had proved abortive earlier was as real a danger as ever. Festus refused to send Paul to Jerusalem, but invited representatives of the hierarchy to appear in Caesarea. Another hearing was held, but the charges against Paul could still not be proved. When Festus refused to release him, Paul, in a last, daring move, appealed to Caesar. In Roman law *appellatio* or the right of appeal was one of the most valuable privileges of citizenship. Paul therefore requested that his case be heard in Rome.

Thus, a political act began to coincide with the progress of the gospel.

Ever since he had been at Ephesus, Paul had felt a compulsion to go to Rome (19:21). All roads in the empire led to Rome. The ecumenical or worldwide faith must sooner or later be proclaimed in the capital of the ecumenical empire. Though Paul was not, of course, the first to preach the gospel in Rome, Luke's account actually ends with a description of Paul's proclamation of the kingdom of God in that city "openly and unhindered." (28:31) Successful though the apostolic mission had been in Judea, Samaria, Asia Minor, and Greece, its very nature demanded that it be brought to the center of world politics.

FOR THOUGHT AND DISCUSSION

The first of the passages to be discussed raises the question of human rights and national self-interest.

God is a God of righteousness, who loves justice. Thus Christians are men of justice. That does not mean that they are "barrack-room lawyers"; it does not mean that they are absorbed in legal formalities, but it means that they are men who are concerned about God's law and justice for men. Justice is not merely what is advantageous to the nation, nor is it just what the nation happens to want: it is only learned by listening to the Word of God. God's Word does not give us a universally valid definition of justice, but it gives us guidance which can help us in a particular instance to determine what is just and to distinguish between right and wrong.

Helmut Gollwitzer, *The Demands of Freedom* [4]

To take an extreme case, is a nation ever free to destroy even one life in order to preserve itself? Most people would say that it is. If it does so destroy, can it do so without being diminished in the process? How does a nation maintain the delicate balance between human rights and the common good? Is this an acute problem in our country today? If so, at what point?

The second passage comes from the Manifesto addressed on Easter 1970 to the Bolivian nation by the Methodist Evangelical Church in Bolivia.

Our best contribution to Bolivia as a Christian Church is to participate in the formation of the new Bolivian man, truly humanized by the gospel of Jesus Christ. . . .

A well-understood evangelization—the proclamation of the Good News and the confrontation of man with the liberating gospel of Jesus Christ—initiates man on the road to his full humanization. But it is necessary to complement that task of proclamation and confrontation with a sustained and systematic effort of education and *conscientization* [making the people aware]. For this reason we consider that the formation of a critical awareness in the Bolivian people and the opening of roads to hope for the marginal citizens of our society is part of the mission which God has entrusted to us. In this sense we assign to the coming massive literacy campaign, to which the government has committed itself, a fundamental role.[5]

Do you agree that social involvement by the church, like the support of a literacy campaign, is part of the mission which God has entrusted to us? What if that involvement meant supporting a revolution against a repressive dictatorship?

The third passage is the only one in the book from a nineteenth-century author. He deals with the subject of Paul's discussion with the procurator Felix.

Old Robbie Flockhart used to say, "It is of no use trying to sew with the silken thread of the gospel unless we pierce a way for it with the sharp needle of the law." The law goes first, like the needle, and draws the gospel thread after it: therefore preach concerning sin, righteousness and judgment to come. . . . Aim at the heart. Probe the wound and touch the very quick of the soul. Spare not the sterner themes, for men must be wounded before they can be healed, and slain before they can be made alive.

Charles H. Spurgeon, *Lectures to My Students* [6]

How do you react to this? Do you agree with the writer that the law is like the needle and draws the gospel thread after it? What do you think he means by saying that men must be wounded before they can be healed? Do you agree with him? Does he agree with Paul?

11

The Sober Madness of a Genius
Acts 25:13—26:32

PAUL'S COURAGE was immense. In its dramatic intensity the scene of the apostle before Agrippa can hardly be surpassed in the history of the church.

In the synagogue at Pisidian Antioch, Paul had declared to the Jews that freedom comes through Christ and not through the law of Moses. In the home of Greek philosophy he had proclaimed what wise men judge absurdity—the resurrection. Near the temple itself he had spoken of his mission to the Gentiles. He had just summoned to the mind of the corrupt Felix the coming judgment. Now he would ask a son of a great Eastern dynasty to hear and obey the truth of Christ. The boldness of the first apostles here came to its climax.

Agrippa invited Paul to make his position clear (26:1). The speech that follows is clearly the edited but authentic voice of the apostle. With his emotions held in check most of the time, Paul retold the story of his conversion. He ended with a strong appeal to the king. It was indeed a brilliant statement, the speech of a genius.

Festus shouted at the end of it, "Paul, you are mad." It took indeed a certain kind of madness to preach with a passion like that, to risk life itself in order to get his message home to the mind of his royal audience. But it was the madness of a genius, a sober madness like that of the first apostles who had drunk deep of the Spirit. Read the whole chapter (26:1–32) and make your own summary of it.

THE THEOLOGY OF A MAN IN CHAINS, 26:1-3

The prisoner on display before Agrippa, Bernice, and their attendants had been in chains since the tribune at Jerusalem had ordered him to be fettered. Like the slaves whom he must have often seen for sale in the markets, Paul himself was now in chains. Indeed, in his Letters he often used the word "slave" to describe himself. He was the slave or servant of Christ, and so he could rejoice in his fetters. But, paradoxically, Christ had freed him from his bondage, and so he was no longer a slave but the freed son of God (Gal. 4:7), and if a son then an heir. Even with the chains of a slave upon him he was a free man.

1) *Salvation as liberation.* Paul wanted the king in front of him to become as he was—*only without chains* (26:29). Here is a deep insight into the gospel. The gospel is always a word and deed of liberation.

The history of black people in America has been one of slavery, so it is not surprising that black theology speaks of salvation as "liberation." To be saved means to be free, to be without chains. Perhaps those whom the world has regarded as slaves now may be the ones who out of their very bondage can teach others how to be free. The salvation of Christ is not simply a spiritual thing. It always works for a future in which the slavery that keeps people from becoming fully alive is wholly done away with. To be saved means to be free, either in fact or in hope. So Christians by their very gospel are part of a "liberation movement."

2) *Christianity as a revolutionary movement.* The true church is the "free church" and the "freeing church." To live by the gospel is to share in the liberation movement by which the glory of God is seen in "man fully alive."

Each age knows something of what this will mean according to its own needs. In the twentieth century the family of man is in bondage to many fears and terrors. The greatest of these is violence. War, unemployment, and disease are expressions of violence done against

man, his dignity, or his body. The good news for us is that God is
the God of love, who takes man's violence to the cross and thereby
declares not that Jesus is condemned but (to use the shorter and
blunter word) that violence itself is damned. Like Paul we are freed
by the cross from the tyrant of the old, violent self and from misdirected love. And we are saved by grace. Being freed, we become
filled with a longing that others too become free—as we are, only
without chains.

Commitment to the Defense of the Gospel, 26:1–3

Paul was the first in a long line of so-called "apologists" (Greek
apologia = defense) committed to explain and defend the Christian
faith to the uncommitted. An apologist is not an apologizer for but
a defender of the gospel.

From the beginning it has been regarded as a necessary task of
the church not only to proclaim but to explain the gospel of Christ.
Peter, for example, counsels his readers to be prepared to have an
answer ready for the people who ask why Christians believe (1 Peter
3:15)—the critics, interested outsiders, or the cultured despisers of
the faith.

What value or meaning will apologetics (the defense of the
gospel) have today? At the least it will mean attempting to explain
our faith in an ever changing situation. Hence the shape of our defense will likely change as each new opportunity comes up. A method
that has worked in one age is not necessarily the best in another. In
the past this defense of the faith was usually addressed to the outsider. Today, because the Christian faith is so seriously questioned
within the church as well as elsewhere, apologetics is more and more
becoming a way of addressing the insider.

We may identify some of the characteristics of a contemporary
defense of the faith. It will be strongly personal, the result of what
has been fashioned in one's own life. It will be "cool," not dogmatic.
It will not boast of having all the answers. Of course it will not
avoid hard questions, but it will not insist that all questions can be
answered. It will not be shocked by contrary opinions. It will be pro-

foundly interested in all human values. Above all, it will seek a commitment to the Christ who is Lord of all. But it will be patient, never trying to force a decision or manipulate any mind.

FAITH AS ENCOUNTER WITH
THE RISEN CHRIST, 26:4–18

Once again Paul told the story of his conversion. For Paul the central reality of faith was the resurrection of Christ, and the Damascus experience was his personal discovery of the risen Lord. For years Paul had brooded on the meaning of what had happened, and his retelling of his conversion was a way of saying two things. First, Christ *is risen*. That is reality. Second, we too can find and enter into that risen life, here and now.

Each person will hear and respond to the proclamation of Christ risen in a different way. But there will be some constants in all our responses.

1) *Sharing the gospel.* One will be to share with others the good news we have heard. We cannot overlook the fact that all the recorded appearances of the risen Christ end with a commission: *go* and *tell*.

2) *Encountering the risen Christ.* A second response will be to discover the risen Christ at times in the least likely places. It is striking that in three of the resurrection appearances in the Gospels Christ is mistaken for someone else—for a gardener by Mary Magdalene (John 20:14–18), for a stranger to the city by the disciples who traveled to Emmaus (Luke 24:13–35), and for a cook preparing a meal by the apostles (John 21:1–14). They did not recognize Christ at first in the ordinary workingman, in the cook, or in the alien. Yet it is in these and their like that we encounter Christ in his risen life.

3) *Resurrection as entrance into new life.* Paul began to know the meaning of the resurrection from his own experience. When he looked back on the old ways—above all the way in which he had ˙

consented to a hate-filled murder (Acts 8:1)—he saw how that old life had been really a dead life, for it was misdirected. But a new thing had happened. He had come to experience a life so full, so intense, and so enjoyable that even an eternity would not be long enough for it. This, Paul saw, is the life and more than life which Christ offers. It is Christ's own life, and the great thing for Paul was that he could enter into it.

In a letter to the author, a young woman who had led a fairly conventional life describes a transformation in her own being after reading a modern book about the Christian faith. She says with some embarrassment that it sounds like "some kookie emotional wingding." It sounds more like an experience of the full, compassionate, and joyful life that Paul knew:

> Something happened. I can only understate it. There is no way to overstate or even to state it. I only know that for an undetermined time I was on my knees in the middle of the living-room floor, experiencing at the depths of my being the healing, accepting love of God. It was all right, in the permission sense, to be me, whatever horrible unspeakable evils that might include. I was released, freed, whole, incredibly grateful, humbled. These in overflowing measure. There is no way to say it. I never believed in it until it happened to me. I still cannot comprehend it. Not even close. The person who said "I" was different from the person who until that moment had said "I." Nothing in my life has ever been the same.

4) *What it means to be good.* In retelling his Damascus experience Paul spoke of his way of life since youth. He had not been an evil man—anything but. Indeed, it had been his misdirected zeal for being in the right that had produced his "raging fury" against the followers of Jesus. But when zeal for any cause produces an explosion of anger like this, we must look very long and critically at the zeal itself.

Paul takes us deep into the heart of his own thinking and into the very springs of morality in two revealing phrases in his writings. In Romans 10:3 he makes a contrast between the righteousness that comes from God and a man's own idea of it. In Philippians 3:9 he contrasts seeking perfection by his own efforts, a perfection based on the law, and the perfection that comes through faith in Christ and is based on faith.

What is at issue in this contrast touches the depths of what it means to be good. One approach is for us to make our minds up in advance that there are certain standards of conduct which are right. We can say that to be truly good means achieving these standards. We can measure our success or failure in achieving these standards. Goodness becomes a matter of what we attain.

Paul's standards before Damacus were clear. They were set out in the books of the Law. If obeying the Law made a man right in the sight of God, then he was faultless. The shattering discovery on the road to Damascus was that this faultless man could become a monster (26:10–11). That way of goodness was not the right one.

Paul's first quest after the Damascus experience was for another way. The answer came to him as a gift, a vision, a disclosure. It was the revelation that we become right in God's sight, that we move toward the perfection God wills for us, not by achieving the standards we choose but by entering into the new life that faith opens up to us. Faith discloses that God loves us despite what we are. Human love may say, "I love you because you are good." God's love says, "I love you, even though you aren't."

Faith (as Paul says) discloses that Jesus is our righteousness. We have no merit, perfection, or goodness of our own. We can only point to him. Faith discloses that God calls us into fellowship with himself, and he welcomes us to his presence because of Jesus.

5) *The effect of this discovery.* No words are large enough to speak of what happens when we make this discovery of God's grace. This other way has a transforming effect on us—we are renewed in our minds. There is a free turning to God made possible by God's invitation to us. There is a liberation from attitudes or policies that dominate us or drive us to hurt or to hate. There is a detachment from self in order to love our neighbor. There is a turning from our past life toward an open and risky future. But there is no fear in this

conversion, because God gives himself to us in it, and God is love, and love casts out fear.

VERDICT OF NOT GUILTY, 26:30–32

After discussing Paul's case with Festus, Agrippa reached his conclusion: This man is not guilty. Had Paul not made his earlier legal appeal, he could now have been set free. It is a strange paradox. Paul could have been freed there and then, free to move on again to a fourth, fifth, or sixth missionary journey. But his very captivity was to be used to advance the gospel.

It is not always best for us to have the freedom we want. It is often better to know how to use our captivity, how to act within limits, how to turn bad events toward a good end. It is bound, limited, or burdened people who often have most to give in the sympathy, sense of unity, and love that build up the human and Christian community. The alcoholic may be "bound," but perhaps he knows more about deep thirsts than most. The divorcee may be burdened, but perhaps she knows a lot about love that we need to learn. The spastic or retarded may be limited, but perhaps he knows more about using limitations to the glory of God than the rest of us. When John Chrysostom, the famed fourth-century preacher, lay dying on the road to the bleak and frigid place to which he had been exiled, he uttered his favorite words: "Glory to God for all things." If we look hard enough we can see a spark for which to praise God in any darkness.

FOR THOUGHT AND DISCUSSION

The first extract to be discussed is based on the argument of the writer that the incarnation means that God binds himself to all human life.

The church must break outside its own institutional, organizational, structural, liturgical, and theological ghettos and be found in identity with the world of men and of their human needs, not in order to do good, not in order to implement a social vision, but precisely in order to find, meet, and know God-in-Christ. The time has come in the history of the church when those of us who are criticized for wanting to get the church mixed up in social problems at the expense of what has traditionally been called "inner spiritual reality" must turn to our critics and meet them on their own ground by saying: "Yes, it is precisely personal salvation that we are talking about when we advocate deep, radical, corporate, and personal involvements in the world of human need. Just like you and with you, what we are talking about is that age-old question, Where does a man meet God and really know him?"

Roger Huber, *No Middle Ground*[1]

The quotation raises a familiar problem. Do you agree that in order to find and know God-in-Christ the church must be found "in identity with human needs"? Would you agree that the God of the Bible is the liberator of his people from their bondage? (Read Luke 1:52–54 and 1:68–75 in a modern translation.) How do you relate personal salvation and involvements in the world of human need? Are we forced to choose one or the other?

There are many religions which know no divine welcome to the sinner until he has ceased to be one. They would first make him righteous, and then bid him welcome to God. But God in Christ first welcomes him, and so makes him penitent and redeems him. The one demands newness of life; the other imparts it. The one demands human righteousness as the price of divine atonement; the other makes atonement in order to evoke righteousness. Christianity brings man to God by bringing God to man. The glory of the Gospel is the free pardon of God, offered to all who will receive it in humble faith.

It was this which amazed Saul of Tarsus. What Johannes Weiss called "this coming of God to meet him," broke him down utterly.

J. S. Whale, *Christian Doctrine*[2]

Do words like these help interpret to you what Paul meant by grace? Can you rewrite them in your own words? How would you describe God's grace to a high school or college youth? How about trying to do it this week?

The third extract is from a letter written by a fifteen-year-old girl. She writes of a shy little girl (herself?) who lived in a distant land. In a quiet forest she saw another human being "for the first time in her life."

> He smiled a smile of acceptance and understanding at her, and suddenly her mouth was full of words. The more words she found, the more she sought. Her whole heart was bursting with happiness, discovery, and love.
>
> When she was with him it was the happiest day in the world. And when she wasn't with him she was smiling back at the sun and listening to the leaves and the birds and kissing the wind and smelling the flowers and looking at everything in the world in wonder and sharing her joy, her love, and her peace with other people. And what's even more exciting, she discovered a whole new world inside herself—a world where sounds came out of silence and colors out of darkness.
>
> Doris Masetti [3]

It is a simple account of falling in love. But it also speaks of a kind of conversion. Do you think Paul's conversion was a kind of falling in love? What insights does this letter give you into Paul's life?

12

Journey's End
Acts 27—28

THE ACTS OF THE APOSTLES ends with the open and unhindered proclamation of the gospel in Rome. But Paul's journey to that city brought him through a danger greater than any he had so far undergone.

THE VOYAGE TO ROME BEGINS, 27:1–3

Travel is usually an exciting experience for us. But travel by sea in Paul's day was frequently tedious and at times terrifying. In the Mediterranean the preferred season for sailing was from March to October. Seafaring in the winter months was very restricted because of the risks.

For the voyage to Rome, Paul was committed with some other prisoners to the charge of a centurion named Julius. Julius seems to have belonged to the special branch of the imperial administration responsible for conveying political prisoners to and from Rome. Paul was possibly in bad health (if he needed to "be cared for"— vs. 3), but Luke was with him (27:1; "we" presumably includes Luke again), and at one of the first ports of call Julius was considerate enough to allow Paul to receive personal attentions from some friends.

A STORM AT SEA, 27:4–44

Weather conditions worsened as the voyage continued. With difficulty the ship reached Fair Havens on the south coast of Crete, but the harbor was not suitable, so the skipper and the ship's owner proposed to move on to better winter quarters at Phoenix.

When they put to sea a gale struck from the northeast. The sails were reefed, the ship's boat, which had been towed behind, was hoisted aboard, and the ship "frapped" or undergirded by passing coils of cable around the hull. Fearing they would be driven on to sandbanks, the seamen lowered a heavy sea anchor to give the ship some stability. But the storm continued unabated, and they were forced to throw overboard most of the cargo and even the spare sails and tackle as well.

After two long and hungry weeks soundings were made which showed the crew of the foundering ship that they were near land. Paul urged the ship's company to eat some food to strengthen themselves for whatever further ordeals might come. The ship stuck fast on a sandbank and began to break apart. At this desperate moment the soldiers who guarded Paul were on the point of killing him, and only the orders of Julius saved him from violent death. Finally, all succeeded in escaping from the broken ship, some by swimming, some on planks.

The absorbing narrative suggests a number of things to us.

1) *Shipwreck and the providence of God.* In reading the account we realize with something like awe how close to death Paul was. Suppose he had gone down with the ship at sea. Was the apostolic community securely enough established and was the gospel widely enough disseminated to survive without him? Probably so. If he had never gotten to Rome, would the growth and expansion of the church have been affected? Again, probably so, and in a number of ways. Paul's contribution to the expansion of early Christianity was unique in the range of his preaching of the Christian message and in his success in gathering together and organizing numbers of believers. An older generation would speak more easily than many of us do of his preservation from death in the shipwreck as the providential intervention of God.

Even though this language is difficult, the passage helps remind us that despite disasters and riddles there *is* such a thing as the purpose of God in history. It is a constant source of surprise that despite storm, invasion, treachery, and carelessnes on the side of man, God continues to hold his world in being. The church also can look at its own past and see how, though its discipleship may have been and still may be timid, and its understanding of his will may have been and still may be fragmentary, God has nevertheless brought it intact to the present. And that is always cause for praise.

2) *Learning how to face a crisis.* There was panic, fear, and even mutiny aboard the ship. It must have been terrifying to face endless days of storm. At any moment the ship might have been shattered like matchwood. Little wonder that some became hysterical and that even the little group around Paul, and indeed the apostle himself, gave up hope of surviving (27:20).

Paul's courage is astonishing. He stood up—not an easy thing to do on a shifting deck—and told them to take courage (27:22). The gospel is heard in different ways according to circumstances. It is heard at various times as a bidding to have faith, to hope, to love, to repent, to be renewed, to be active, to rest. Here it is heard as a word of encouragement.

Early in the morning, before the ship's company buffeted the waves to get ashore on pieces of wreckage, Paul ate a hasty meal with them. He took some bread, gave thanks to God, and began to eat (27:35). It was typical of Paul that the man who could sing hymns of praise to God at midnight in a Philippian jail would bear witness to the God whose purpose even storms cannot frustrate.

3) *The need to hold together.* The description of the shipwreck also points to a truth the deeper meaning of which Paul develops in First Corinthians—the need of the commuity to hold together.

When he saw some of the crew trying to escape in the ship's boat, Paul warned the centurion that the loss of the few might mean calamity for all (27:31). In his Letter to the Corinthians Paul deals with the same idea, though in a different connection and at a deeper level. The human body is made up of many parts, each with a purpose and each indispensable. No part can function well without the others (1 Cor. 12:12–30). His words are important in regard not only to the church but also to the broader human community.

There is considerable talk today about division in the church. Would it not be better, it is suggested, if the liberals and ecumenists went their way, leaving the conservatives to remain loyal to their traditions? In the broader human community recall the often tense relations between suburbs and the inner city. To each community Paul has still a word to say: we need each other. When some try to escape there may be calamities for all.

Arrival at Rome, 28:1–14

In the spring after the shipwreck the last stage of the journey was begun. In a ship bearing the figures of Castor and Pollux, the patrons of sailors, on its prow, Paul and his companions voyaged from Malta and landed on the Italian mainland at Puteoli.

"And so we came to Rome"—with these simple words a new chapter in Rome's history, and the history of Europe, begins. The empire had many large cities, teeming centers of mixed populations and widely differing cultural and religious life. Above and beyond them all stood Rome. It was built on the famous hills. Its vast walls made it a fortress. Its temples and monuments were reminders of its ancient faith and present grandeur. Tenement houses, many of them squalid, were thronged with crowds from every nation. In Paul's day the population was close to 700,000.

Rome in a sense is the mother of us all. Through her have come to us not only the glory that was Greece and the grandeur that was Rome but also the faith of the apostolic church; not only all that is true, or noble, or good, or honorable out of the classical world, but also the belief that the personal and holy God has called the world to become the new creation in Christ.

The Gospel Is Preached in Rome, 28:15–31

Paul arrived in Rome probably in A.D. 60 or 61. He was given a warm welcome by the members of the Christian community and permitted by the authorities to take up residence under guard in a private dwelling. Contacts were made with local leaders of the synagogue. To these Paul explained his position and his faith. He had never been disloyal to the old religion. He simply wanted to show how Israel's hopes are fulfilled in Jesus Christ. In all his teachings Paul's theme remains constant: the kingdom of God and the Lordship of Christ (28:23).

For two years, according to Luke, Paul continued his apostolic work, teaching his gospel with all the old conviction. We do not hear of his death in Acts. We do not *know* anything of what happened to him after this. There is a hint in a document written toward the end of the first century. The writer, a bishop of Rome called Clement, says: "He taught righteousness to the whole world and went to the western limit of the earth." Does this mean that Paul went to Spain? He wrote to the Romans that he hoped to see them on his way to Spain (Rom. 15:24). But it seems unlikely that Paul ever went that far. No other writer refers to such a journey.

So Acts closes with almost intolerable abruptness. It is like losing the last chapter in a biography. What happened to Paul, to the young community in Rome? We are anxious to know, but Luke is silent. All he tells us is that the Christian faith, born in an obscure part of the empire, was finally proclaimed in the capital itself by the apostle to the Gentiles.

What came after Paul's entry into Rome is really a new beginning. In a profound sense every "end" in the movement of the people of God is also a new beginning. In the words of a modern writer, "the whole history of the church is a succession of beginnings." [1] Another way to put it is that the acts of apostolic men and women are still being done throughout the world.

FOR THOUGHT AND DISCUSSION

The first extract discusses the problem of providence.

The Christian style of life is built around a biblical realism that looks at life unblinking, that sees it for the castle perilous it really is, that reacts to its frustrations and dangers with a faith that lets honest fear teach men humility and compassion *in community*. The really "stylish" Christian takes it for granted that existence is tenuous and untoward—the nice guys do often finish last, if they aren't finished off first. . . . He sees his joys and sorrows in the perspective of life as a training ground for growing persons—all of it provided and cared for by grace. . . .

But the life of grace that lives fully in the present is also life open to the future and to death. For all that life means now must really await judgment as to what it will have meant when it can all be seen in just perspective. For the Christian, this turns on his faith in God's providence for the human future as well as the past. Such a faith knows as well as any sceptic that our proximate futures are inscrutable and that our final future is, literally, inconceivable. But it does believe that God's providence for our freedom, identity and power to love will continue to "the end" as it has from "the beginning."

Albert C. Outler, *Who Trusts in God* [2]

Do the writer's realism and honesty make the concept of providence more understandable and acceptable to you? Looking back over the past two or three months, what evidence do you see of God's providence? If you see none, what kind of evidence would convince you of his providential care? Try to relate your answers and the quotation above to Paul's experience in the shipwreck.

The second passage speaks of the meaning and source of courage at a time of crisis. The author is a pastor in East Germany.

Of course, one meets many pastors among us who are tired and resigned. Since 1945 a number of us have moved west, and many fewer have come our way. . . . Here we live from week to week on his [God's] comfort and guidance. Here he drives us continually to the point where there is nothing else we can do but plead and ask for his grace. And still we so often complain and yearn for those earthly gifts, small and large, which he gives us at the moment in short supply or perhaps denies us altogether and which we find it so hard to do without.

I think here not only of food and clothing, shoes and medicine (here you help us with great faithfulness and love). I do not think first of all of books, magazines and newspapers, the dearth of which shuts us out more and more from your world of the mind. I think first of all of that bit of freedom and justice by which the individual is protected against the arbitrary misuse of state power. Security before the law is a tremendous thing, but our flesh, our old Adam, confuses it so easily with the one thing which is absolutely necessary! The man who believes can no longer live without the gathering of the brethren around the Word and the Lord's Table. But he can, if need be, endure the plunder of his possessions with joy (Heb. 10:34). He can, like Paul and Silas, praise God in the stocks at midnight, so that the fellow-prisoners hear (Acts 16:25 ff.). He who does not believe places his hope and his confidence in this or that condition of this life. He loses himself therein and despairs when life disappoints him. But those who form the "third race" know that we must enter the Kingdom of God through much suffering. And precisely therein they come to realize by a wealth of experience that our Father in Heaven knows what our needs are.

Johannes Hamel, *A Christian in East Germany* [3]

In what ways does the German pastor remind you of the first apostles? What does he regard as the one thing necessary? What encouragement does he find in the political crisis of his land? How can Christians in different circumstances reach the same *certainty* "that our Father . . . knows what our needs are"?

Author, Purpose, and Date

T HE GOSPEL OF LUKE and the Acts of the Apostles are two parts
of a composite work. Tradition has always spoken of the author
as Luke. Together the Gospel and Acts are larger than all the surviving Letters of Paul. Luke has thus written more of the New
Testament than any other writer.

He is an artist in words. His story of the birth of Jesus and his
record of the parables of the lost sheep, the lost coin, and the prodi-
gal son have deeply colored our understanding of the gospel. Only
Luke records the saying that the Son of man came to seek and save
what is lost. Only Luke tells us about Zacchaeus and of the promise
to the thief on the cross.

Acts has similarly helped shape our understanding of the church.
It is the most important single source of our knowledge of the early
church and has been described (a little extravagantly) as "the most
popular historical work the world has ever seen." [1]

THE AUTHOR

Luke was a companion of Paul, who called him "the beloved
physician." (Col. 4:14) In the second century A.D. several pieces
of evidence name him as the author of Acts. The so-called Mura-
torian Canon says: "Moreover the Acts of all the apostles are included in one book. Luke addressed them to the most excellent
Theophilus, because the several events took place when he was
present." [2] While there is some doubt about the second part of the

statement, clearly from early days Luke was regarded as the author of Acts.

Several passages in the second half of the book refer to "we" instead of the more usual "they" in designating the companions of Paul. The most natural conclusion is that the "we" includes Luke, and, if so, we can assume that he was in Paul's company for most of the time on his last journeys. It seems a safe conclusion that the author of the "we" sections also wrote the rest of the book.

It is only fair to say that not all Biblical scholars today agree with this conclusion. Any good commentary or Bible dictionary can provide the arguments pro and con if you wish to go further into this issue.

LUKE'S SOURCES

Luke is a careful historian. In his preface to the Gospel he says that he has tried to give an accurate account (Luke 1:2). The sources of his history in Acts are many. He was a close companion of Paul. He had shared with him the rigors of long travels. He knew many in the cities of Jerusalem, Antioch, and Caesarea. He may have known John Mark, who is mentioned in 12:12 and who may be the author of the second Gospel. Many records circulated in the early church about its first leaders, and Luke with his inquiring mind may have consulted them.

THE TITLE

In the earliest manuscripts of the New Testament the book is named in Greek *praxeis ton apostolon,* Acts of the Apostles. The omission of the familiar definite article suggests that what follows is a selection, chosen with care, of certain episodes only ("Some Acts," not "The Acts," so to speak).

Suppose that you had just a few pages on which to give an account of your life to date. You would hardly begin and end the report of each day by writing: got up, went to bed. A friend of the present author wrote a brief history of the church for junior highs.

To do so he carefully selected forty-nine episodes from two thousand years, each because it gave its distinctive color to the total picture.

Luke knew that if everything the apostles did were to be written, the largest library could hardly contain the books. As in the case of the Gospel he tried to confine himself to the limits of a single roll of papyrus. These expensive rolls usually did not exceed about thirty feet in length. Luke had therefore to be very selective. When he repeated a story (three times in the case of Saul's conversion) he showed how central it was to his account.

Luke's Purpose

Luke wrote Acts for many reasons. He wanted to show what Christian belief is and what effects it has. He sought to describe what God had done through the apostles and in the earliest communities of believers. He wanted to show that the expansion of the church had come about through the activity of God. God was in control, establishing his kingdom, and the good news was beginning to be proclaimed to the ends of the earth. Through the power of his Spirit the gospel had been brought even to Rome itself, despite opposition and danger. (Additional brief, helpful comments on Luke's purpose can be found in Winn's *Acts of the Apostles,* LBC, vol. 20, pp. 11–14.)

Luke as a Writer and Historian

Luke is a superb writer. With an easy, fluent style he puts words together to form the most literary part of the New Testament.

He is also a competent historian. Though parts of his account are difficult to square with Paul at times (see below), his careful respect for details shows that he is a writer who is familiar with his sources. For instance, he accurately describes the distinctions between officials of the empire. Many of these distinctions would be quite confusing to the general public.

Luke is not just a historian of the church. He has a view of history in which he holds together the purposeful activity of God and the political community of the Roman Empire. This makes his record very valuable to us when we in our time try to interpret God's action in history.

THE SPEECHES IN ACTS

Today tape and film reproduce exactly what the microphone picks up or the camera views. We expect reporters and historians to record what was said or done with strict accuracy.

In ancient histories it was not the custom to do things this way. Though shorthand was known and used in the classical world, a historian tried to express the gist or the spirit of what was said on momentous occasions, rather than the exact words.

A typical representative of this attitude was the Greek historian Thucydides, author of a famous history of the war between Athens and Sparta. Referring to the speeches of those who were involved in the war, he says: "My habit has been to make the speakers say what was in my opinion demanded of them by the occasion, of course adhering as closely as possible to the general sense of what they really said."

The speeches in Acts, especially those of Peter and Paul, but also those of Gamaliel, Stephen, and others, are not a word for word rendering of what was said. Their very brevity shows this. They are summaries, giving a general idea. Yet when we compare the style of the speeches with the rest of the narrative, we find that they are less polished. So it is likely that in many instances Luke is giving us a fairly accurate transcription of what was said by the speaker.

LUKE AND PAUL AT VARIANCE WITH EACH OTHER

A close comparison of Acts and the Letters of Paul will show descriptions of the same episode or circumstance apparently at variance with one another. For instance, Paul openly speaks of the dangers of introducing "another gospel." Attempts to force circumcision on converts would produce a grave crisis in the church. Luke in contrast, though not silent about the crisis, tends to play it down in what has been called "an unduly peaceful picture."

The explanation is probably that Paul is dealing in his Letters with immediate problems in the local community of believers. Luke is reflecting upon the past and trying to show how the achievement of unity and the principle of salvation by grace were undeniably present in the church from the beginning.

DATE

Paul's two years of detention in Rome (Acts 28:30) took place about A.D. 61 to 63. This gives us one limit for dating Acts—it was written after A.D. 63. Some scholars have held that Acts was written *much* later, say about A.D. 120, and that it is a kind of rewriting of history in the interests of a particular outlook.

We know that by about A.D. 95 Paul's Letters were being widely circulated and exercising considerable authority in the church. It has been suggested that it was the publication of Acts that was responsible for bringing the stature of Paul and his massive contribution to the fore. This would mean that Acts appeared shortly before, say between A.D. 80 and 90. Most scholars would accept this approximate date, or perhaps sometime between A.D. 70 and 90.

Notes

CHAPTER 1

1. R. R. Williams, *The Acts of the Apostles* (London: SCM Press, 1953), p. 26. Used by permission.
2. R. A. Knox, *Enthusiasm,* p. 591. Used by permission of The Clarendon Press, Oxford.
3. John A. T. Robinson, *But That I Can't Believe!* (New York: The New American Library, 1967), p. 58. Used by permission.
4. From *God's Frozen People,* by Mark Gibbs & T. Ralph Morton, The Westminster Press. © 1964 by Mark Gibbs & T. Ralph Morton. © 1965 by W. L. Jenkins. Used by permission.

CHAPTER 2

1. From *The Jerusalem Bible,* copyright © 1966 by Darton, Longman & Todd, Ltd. and Doubleday & Company, Inc.
2. *The Didache,* ch. 9. This anonymous document was probably written in the first century A.D.
3. John S. Whale, *Christian Reunion: Historic Divisions Reconsidered* (Grand Rapids, Michigan: William B. Eerdmans Publishing Company, 1971), pp. 36–37. Used by permission.
4. William Barclay, *Ethics in a Permissive Society* (London and Glasgow: Collins Fontana Books, 1971), p. 167. Used by permission.
5. "The Death of God and the End of History," Thomas Merton, *Theoria to Theory,* Vol. II, First Quarter (October 1967), p. 11. Used by permission.

CHAPTER 3

1. From the terms of the William Monroe Wicker Award, an award made to Union Theological Seminary in Virginia by the Adult Fellowship Class of the First Presbyterian Church, Charlotte, North Carolina. Wicker was a former student at Union Seminary and was killed in action in World War II.
2. Konrad Lorenz, *On Aggression,* tr. Marjorie Kerr Wilson (New York: Harcourt, Brace & World, Inc., 1966), pp. 215, 217. Used by permission.
3. Rosemary Ruether, "Ministry in the Church of the Future," Gerard S. Sloyan, ed., *Secular Priest in the New Church* (New York: Herder and Herder, 1967), pp. 136, 146 f. Used by permission.
4. From "Organized Torture in Brazil," *IDOC-North America* No. 5, June 13, 1970, pp. 2–19. Used by permission.
5. "On Being and Being Black," Etheridge Knight, *Black Lines,* Vol. I, No. 1 (October 1970), pp. 15 f. Used by permission.

CHAPTER 4

1. W. R. Forrester, *Conversion* (Edinburgh: The St. Andrew Press, 1956), pp. 13, 15. Used by permission.

2. J. Glenn Gray, *The Warriors: Reflections on Men in Battle* (New York: Harper & Row, 1967), pp. 175 f. The author is Professor of Philosophy, Colorado College, Colorado Springs, Colorado 80903. Used by permission.
3. Dag Hammarskjöld, *Markings*, tr. Leif Sjöberg and W. H. Auden (New York: Alfred A. Knopf, 1964), p. 205. Used by permission.

CHAPTER 5

1. Philip Carrington, *The Early Christian Church* (Cambridge: Cambridge University Press, 1957), p. 64. Used by permission.
2. From "The Freedom of a Christian" in Theodore G. Tappert, ed., *The Selected Writings of Martin Luther, 1520–1523* (Philadelphia: Fortress Press, p. 20). © 1967 by Fortress Press and reprinted with the permission of the publisher.
3. From *Why Black Power?* By Joseph R. Barndt. Copyright Friendship Press, New York 1968, pp. 121–122. Used by permission.
4. From *Situation Ethics,* by Joseph Fletcher. The Westminster Press, Philadelphia 1966, pp. 45, 61. Copyright © W. L. Jenkins. Used by permission.
5. "Dialogue and Its Philosophy," Dominque Dubarle, *Concurrence,* No. 1 (Winter 1969), p. 8. Used by permission.

CHAPTER 6

1. T. E. Lawrence, *Seven Pillars of Wisdom* (Garden City, New York: Doubleday, Doran & Company, Inc., 1936), p. 339.
2. E. H. Robertson, *Christians Against Hitler* (London: SCM Press, 1962), p. 84.
3. Kevin and Dorothy Ranaghan, *As the Spirit Leads Us* (Paramus, New Jersey: Paulist Press, 1971), pp. 9–10. Used by permission.
4. *The Creator Spirit in Secular Society,* Reports of Task Forces, North American Area Council, The World Alliance of Reformed and Presbyterian Churches (January 12, 1966), p. 45 f. Used by permission.
5. "The New Violence," Joseph Morgenstern, Copyright *Newsweek,* Inc. (February 14, 1972), p. 69. Used by permission.

CHAPTER 7

1. "Look Ahead America," Howard E. Kershner, *Christian Economics* (September 1971), p. 6 Used by permission.
2. "Does the U.S. Exploit the Developing Nations?" David S. French, *Commonweal* (May 19, 1967), pp. 257–259. Used by permission.
3. Daniel Berrigan, *No Bars to Manhood* (Garden City, New York: Doubleday & Co., Inc., 1970), pp. 114–115.
4. Kenneth Clark, *Civilisation: A Personal View* (New York: Harper & Row, 1969), pp. 346–347. Used by permission.

CHAPTER 8

1. Joy Davidman, *Smoke on the Mountain: The Ten Commandments in Terms of Today* (London: Hodder & Stoughton, 1955), pp. 30–39.
2. Hans J. Hillerbrand, *The Reformation* (New York: Harper & Row, 1964), pp. 42–43. Used by permission.

3. Walter de la Mare, "Fare Well," in *Collected Poems* (New York: H. Holt & Company, 1941). Used by permission.
4. George Elton Ladd, *Jesus and the Kingdom: The Eschatology of Biblical Realism* (New York: Harper & Row, 1964), p. 273. Used by permission.
5. "The Political Economy of War," Douglas F. Dowd, *The Nation* (June 28, 1971), p. 813. Used by permission.
6. From *The Future of the Christian Sunday* by Christopher Kiesling, © Sheed and Ward, Inc., 1970, pp. 139–140. Used by permission.

CHAPTER 9

1. *John Knox's History of the Reformation in Scotland*, ed. W. Croft Dickinson, Vol. I (London: Thomas Nelson & Sons, Ltd., 1949), p. 182. Used by permission.
2. Karl Heim, *The World: Its Creation and Consummation* (Edinburgh: Oliver & Boyd, 1962), pp. 134 f. Used by permission.
3. From *Prayers* by Michel Quoist, © Sheed & Ward Inc., 1963, pp. 65–66. Used by permission.
4. Hans Toch, *Violent Men: An Inquiry into the Psychology of Violence* (Chicago: Aldine Publishing Company, 1969), pp. 209–211. The quotation used is from *Rivers of Blood, Years of Darkness* by Robert Conot. Copyright © 1967 by Bantam Books, Inc. Both used by permission.

CHAPTER 10.

1. From *Luther and His Times* by E. G. Schwiebert, copyright in 1950 by Concordia Publishing House, p. 499. Used by permission.
2. From *Calvin: Institutes of the Christian Religion*, Vol. XXI, The Library of Christian Classics, edited by John T. McNeill and translated by Ford Lewis Battles. Published in the U.S.A. by The Westminster Press. Copyright MCMLX, by W. L. Jenkins. Used by permission.
3. "I Felt the Split Coming," Copyright: *Life* Magazine, © 1971 Time, Inc. Used by permission.
4. Helmut Gollwitzer, *The Demands of Freedom*, tr. Robert W. Fenn (New York: Harper & Row, 1965), p. 67. Used by permission.
5. From "The Methodist Manifesto to the Bolivian Nation," *IDOC-North America* No. 7, July 18, 1970, pp. 39–48. Used by permission.
6. Charles H. Spurgeon, *Lectures to My Students* (London: Marshall, Morgan & Scott, 1954), p. 338. Used by permission.

CHAPTER 11

1. Roger Huber, *No Middle Ground* (Nashville: Abingdon Press, 1971), p. 70. Used by permission.
2. J. S. Whale, *Christian Doctrine* (Cambridge: Cambridge University Press, 1950), pp. 78–79. Used by permission.
3. Quoted with permission from a letter to a friend.

CHAPTER 12

1. R. B. Rackham, *The Acts of the Apostles* (London: Methuen & Co., Ltd., 1957), p. 507. Used by permission.

2. Albert C. Outler, *Who Trusts in God: Musings on the Meaning of Providence* (New York: Oxford University Press, 1968), pp. 124–125. Used by permission.
3. Johannes Hamel, *A Christian in East Germany,* tr. Ruth and Charles C. West (London: SCM Press, 1960), p. 31 f. Used by permission.

APPENDIX

1. *Early Christianity: The Purpose of Acts and Other Papers,* ed. Frederick C. Grant (Greenwich, Connecticut: Seabury Press, 1954), p. 41. Used by permission.
2. *Documents of the Christian Church,* ed. Henry Bettenson (London: Oxford University Press, 1963), p. 28. Used by permission.

Other Titles in the
BIBLE STUDIES FOR MODERN MAN
Series

The Covenants in Faith and History   *Stephen Szikszai*

A chain of covenants binds together the history of the people of God in the Old and New Testaments. In this book Stephen Szikszai describes six crucial covenant-making events recorded in the Bible. The first is the covenant with Moses at Mt. Sinai. Significant occasions of covenant renewal took place in the times of Joshua, David, Josiah, and Ezra. The series of covenants came to a climax in the New Covenant of Jesus Christ and the formation of God's new people, the church. Covenant renewal continues in the church through worship and sacrament. The task of the people of God in the Bible and in today's church is the healing of mankind.

Exercises in Interpreting Scripture   *John Frederick Jansen*

There are many books for laymen about the Bible, but this short volume is unique. It is not only an introduction to the study of the Bible but a book that helps the layman develop his skills of interpretation. After outlining the interpreter's task, with all its pitfalls and opportunities, Dr. Jansen carries the reader another step. He helps him interpret four Bible passages that raise the kinds of problems found throughout Scripture. Each passage is examined in terms of what it meant in the context of its times and in the context of the larger portion of Scripture of which it is a part. The author then moves to the question of what the passage means in today's world.

Leader's Guide to   *Mac N. and*
Bible Studies for Modern Man   *Anne Shaw Turnage*

These session-by-session helps are for those who lead adults or older youth in the study of the three books in the Bible Studies for Modern Man series.